AMAZING GIRLS OF ARIZONA

Christmas 2009

We hope this gets you
interested in Arizona so
you bring your parents
to visit us there!

Love,
Uncle Al
&
Aunt Jitz
♡

AMAZING GIRLS OF ARIZONA

True Stories of Young Pioneers

JAN CLEERE

TWODOT®

GUILFORD, CONNECTICUT
HELENA, MONTANA

AN IMPRINT OF THE GLOBE PEQUOT PRESS

A · TWODOT® · BOOK

Copyright © 2008 Morris Book Publishing, LLC

Text design: Debbie V. Nicolais

Front cover photo: Edith Jane Bass feeding the chickens, 1910. Image courtesy of Cline Library, Northern Arizona University.

Credits for the photographs that appear with each chapter can be found on page 185.

Library of Congress Cataloging-in-Publication Data is available.
ISBN 978-0-7627-4135-9

Manufactured in the United States of America
First Edition/Second Printing

To my daughter Sue,
an amazing girl, a remarkable woman.

CONTENTS

INTRODUCTION

"Children are our most valuable resource," according to the thirty-first President of the United States, Herbert Clark Hoover (1929–1933). Nowhere was this adage truer than along westward trails and in rustic homes first established by pioneering families. Children were necessary workers who helped with the many chores associated with maintaining a covered wagon on the long trek across the Plains, or the duties and responsibilities of running a ranch or farm in the growing Southwest.

Girls from a very early age were expected to care for younger children, wash clothes and dishes, cook and clean, feed the poultry and pigs, milk the cows, administer to sick animals, and tend the gardens. They helped mend fences, round up wandering herds, and repair dried-up water holes. According to Cathy Luchetti, author of *Children of the West: Family Life on the Frontier*, "Girls were slated to tend the familial home first, their own futures second, and according to their responsibilities, their behavior was closely monitored."

Yet even as early as the 1800s, girls strained against the confines of housework and home chores, particularly those who came west with their families and saw the possibilities and potential of conquering new lands and new beginnings.

They tossed off their restrictive sunbonnets that allowed limited vision, and rode pell-mell across the vast countryside. They watched the sun rise and set as they stoked the campfire on a cattle drive. They learned to wrangle a calf and break a horse, and reveled in the beauty of the desert as they rode out to repair fences, farm the land, and tend the stock. They discovered and embraced the new world that lay before them.

A number of their feats were truly amazing, even astounding. Not just because they were little girls, but also because they met head-on life's most demanding and difficult experiences.

Early Arizona girls faced unique challenges—unbelievable heat, lack of water, strange foods, dangerous animals, and uprooted Native Indians. They learned to cope with the heat, preserve precious water, savor new victuals, avoid and defend themselves from lurking predators. But most of all, they conquered the dangers and difficulties encountered in their daily lives.

The beauty of the Arizona desert, its lush high-mesa plains and snowcapped northern mountains, brought out creative possibilities in young girls as they painted and wrote of the spell the wild territory cast over their lives.

Girls penned letters, journals, and diaries, describing their tears of hardships and heartaches, their dreams of greatness and love. They spoke of Indian massacres and captivity, imprisonment and banishment. They complained about endless chores and squabbling younger siblings. And they boasted of unrewarded accomplishments and prohibited misdeeds. The passage of time has not dimmed their ordeals and achievements. Interspersed with historic details, the earnest stories of these sometimes brave, often heroic young girls have survived the passage of time to be told and retold, with their own words.

INTRODUCTION

Even as time passed and the territory changed, Arizona girls continued to challenge, overcome, and surmount new obstacles and difficulties.

As the country advanced into the twentieth century, Arizona girls encountered even more possibilities as they entered firehouses and police stations, rode on rockets soaring to the moon, and brought a new meaning to the term "Play Ball!" as they took to sports fields and arenas previously off limits.

Today, very little stands in the way of a young girl's dreams. She enjoys freedom of choice and opportunity because her great-grandmother determined she would not bow to the Victorian rigidity and rules of nineteenth-century conformity and compliance. Perhaps her grandmother burned her bra during the women's movement of the 1960s to ensure her own daughter could drive a racecar or ride a bucking bronco, own and run her own business or become president and C.E.O. of a conglomerate, or face the enemy on the warfront.

I can only imagine what new vistas tomorrow's Arizona girls will discover, explore, defeat, and conquer.

INDIAN CAPTIVE

Olive Ann Oatman (Fairchild)
1837–1903

With each barefoot step, Olive Ann Oatman felt the stab
of an Indian's lance provoking her to move faster. Tightly
clutching her little sister's hand, she tried to quiet the
child's sobs of fright and pain as the Indians hurried the
two girls across the rock-strewn desert. Mary Ann's tiny
footsteps left a bloody path as both girls struggled to
maintain the unrelenting pace their captors demanded.
Farther and farther they traveled, miles from where their
abductors had brutally attacked the Oatman family. From
the horrors Olive and Mary Ann witnessed, they feared
their entire family now lay dead or dying.

Thirteen-year-old Olive did not know what fate awaited her and eight-year-old Mary Ann, but during the ensuing terrifying days, she found herself wishing she might also end up lying beside their parents and five siblings along the banks of the Gila River, deep within Arizona Territory.

Olive had been excited about the adventure that lay before her family as she helped her mother prepare for the long journey from Illinois to the promised land of Bashan that James Colin Brewster, who had broken from Brigham Young's Mormon teachings, touted as the land of golden opportunity. In 1846, Young had called his people to follow him to Utah. In 1849, Brewster ordered his followers to prepare for the journey to what he described as the real Zion located at the confluence of the Gila and Colorado Rivers, across the desolate and dangerous Southwestern desert. In the summer of 1850, with his farm failing to provide for his growing family, Roys Oatman, Olive's father, led his wife Mary Ann and their seven children across the Mississippi River to join other Brewsterites in Independence, Missouri. From there, the wagon train headed west.

The trip was long and arduous, but the travelers

remained a cohesive group until
October when their wagons rum-
bled into New Mexico Territory.
By then, dissension was brewing
among the homesteaders.

Unable to resolve their differences,
one group led by Brewster headed toward Santa Fe while
the Oatmans hitched their wagons to the contingent
going by way of the Rio Grande Valley. Awed by the
stark beauty of the surrounding desert, Olive was also old
enough to understand the dangers she and her family
might encounter along this unfamiliar path. A lack of
food already made the travelers disgruntled and tense.
Now they faced the possibility of Indian attacks as they
crossed into hostile Apache territory.

On January 8, 1851, the Oatmans and the rest of the
party arrived in the dusty Mexican town of Tucson. It
would take an act of Congress in 1854 to ratify the
Gadsden Purchase and make Tucson, along with land
south of the Gila River, part of the United States. Even
then, this region remained part of New Mexico Territory
until 1863 when the Territory of Arizona was finally
established.

In dire need of food and supplies before continuing their journey across the heart of the Southwestern desert, the straggling travelers found no provisions in Tucson. Scant rain had fallen during the past winter, drying up what crops the Apaches had not ransacked and ravished. The townspeople were hard put to feed themselves.

Olive, along with her older sister Lucy, kept watch over the younger Oatman children while the adults considered their next course of action. Olive was most worried about little Mary Ann, named after her mother, who had never been as healthy as the other children. She had no such worries about her strapping fourteen-year-old brother Lorenzo who was already more man than boy.

Again the group split into two factions with one group choosing to stay in Tucson until they could buy or produce enough food for the journey west. The other party, including the Oatmans, headed north about ninety miles to Maricopa Wells where they hoped friendly Pima and Maricopa tribes might spare essential supplies for the desert crossing. They still had over two hundred treacherous miles to go before reaching the banks of the Colorado River.

But there was no food to spare in the drought-stricken tribal villages.

While in Maricopa Wells, Roys
Oatman met John Lawrence LeConte,
considered one of the foremost ento-
mologists of the nineteenth century,
and an expert in the study and identifi-
cation of beetles. LeConte was on an
expedition to explore the Colorado
River area and study the insects of the
Southwest. He and his guide had just
traveled the span of desert from the army
encampment at Yuma, situated on the shores
of the Colorado River. Not once, LeConte proclaimed,
had he seen any hostile Indians along the way. Several
tribes occupied or traveled the land between Maricopa
Wells and the Colorado River, including the numerous
Western Apaches and the lesser-known Yavapai tribes.

While the rest of the homesteaders chose to remain in
Maricopa Wells until they could acquire much-needed
supplies, Roys Oatman, relying on LeConte's declaration
that he would not encounter renegade Indians, readied
his family for the strenuous trip across the desert. With
his wife one month away from giving birth to their

eighth child, he might have felt she would be safer within the confines Camp Yuma than in an ancient Indian village.

On February 10, 1851, with scant food, four skinny cows, and one wagon pulled by a couple of starving oxen, the Oatmans headed out alone, following the Gila River toward the Colorado River. The way was exceedingly rough, the family already exhausted from lack of food and the long journey already endured.

Each day they faced steep hills that had to be climbed, only to discover another rise on the other side. Because the emaciated oxen, burdened with the weighty wagon containing all their possessions, balked at scrambling up the precipitous prominences, the family emptied the wagon and toted their belongings up each hill. They then had to put everything back into the wagon before starting out again. They rarely conquered more than one hill a day.

After six days on their own, Olive and the rest of the family were overjoyed when James LeConte, on his way back to Camp Yuma, stopped by their meager campsite. Seeing the desperation of the Oatmans, LeConte told the family he would ride ahead and send a party of soldiers to escort them the rest of the way. Grateful, the Oatmans watched the entomologist ride away, believing their woeful journey almost at an end.

LeConte, however, only traveled a few miles before a small band of Indians accosted him and took off with his horse and that of his guide. Fearing the Oatmans might encounter the same Indians, he tacked a note on a nearby tree warning of the danger before hurrying on toward Yuma. He could only pray the Oatmans found his note.

The next day, February 18, the family rose to face yet another sheer incline. All day they toted their possessions up the bluff that rose above the Gila River. Finally, with everything again in place, the exhausted family sat down to supper—a weak pot of soup sopped up with small pieces of bread. They ate ravenously, too tired to complain about the meager feast.

From out of nowhere the Indians appeared and approached the bedraggled family. Begging for food, the half-starved band accepted the Oatman's paltry offerings, then demanded more. But with over eighty miles yet to go, the family could spare no more.

Without warning, the Indians attacked. Olive watched horrified as first her older brother Lorenzo fell from a vicious blow to the head. Next her father, then her mother with baby Roland in her arms, were brutally beaten to the ground. One by one, she witnessed her sisters Lucy and Charity, and little Roys Jr., drop lifeless onto the rock-hard earth. Only she and Mary Ann remained standing, the Indians forcing them away from the blood-soaked landscape.

Neither girl had time to mourn the outcome of the gruesome acts they had witnessed. Hurried off barefoot and bewildered, across unfamiliar barren lands, terrified of what dreadful fate might await them, they dared not even speak to each other.

Olive always thought her captors were raiding Apaches who readily attacked for sport, but in all probability the Indians who descended upon the lone wagon came from one of the nearby Yavapai tribes, although no proof exists confirming which tribe the warriors represented.

Hour after hour the girls stumbled over sharp rocks that left their feet bleeding profusely. For nourishment, they were offered food from their own wagon. Neither sister could eat the ill-gotten rations. Later, Olive recorded her memories in the book, *Captivity of the Oatman Girls*:

> *The Indians took off their packs, struck a fire, and began in their own way to make preparations for a meal. They boiled some of the beans just from our wagon, mixed some flour with water, and baked it in the ashes. They offered us some food, but in the most insulting and taunting manner, continually making merry over every indication of grief in us, and with which our hearts were ready to break. We could not eat. After the meal, and about an hour's rest, they began to repack and make preparations to proceed.*

Once again on the move, Olive steeled herself against the agony of the forced march. But little Mary Ann soon weakened. Each time the child fell, she was beaten until she rose and willed herself to continue. Eventually, she could go no farther and one of the Indians hauled the little girl up on his back while prodding Olive to move even faster.

The group continued across the almost treeless desert, ever under the blinding glare of an unrelenting sun. Olive tended to Mary Ann as best she could, but she had no means to alleviate her sister's pain and anguish. "We thought they would kill us and hoped they would do so," she remembered.

After three or four days, a village appeared on the horizon that Olive later described as "a cluster of low, thatched huts, each having an opening near the ground." Here she and Mary Ann spent the next year as slaves— ridiculed, beaten, and starved to the point of death, but always left alive enough to do the bidding of their new masters.

They were forced to carry heavy loads and whipped if they dropped their burdens. Even the smallest children taunted and teased, poked and jabbed, forcing the two girls to do their bidding.

For food they had to fend for themselves. Mesquite beans, grass seed, roots, and tree bark were mainstays. What little meat was brought into the camp never made it to Olive and Mary Ann's plates. The past winter, devoid of rain to nourish the crops, had left the entire tribe suffering from lack of food.

Olive numbly went about her tasks, avoiding those who enjoyed lashing out at her. She tried to shield frail Mary Ann as best she could, but her sister suffered terribly that first year.

Occasionally, a group of Mohave Indians visited the camp bringing much-needed vegetables and grains, which they exchanged for furs and animal skins. The Mohaves became interested in the two white girls and began bargaining for them, finally purchasing Olive and Mary Ann for three blankets, two horses, some vegetables, and a handful of beads. The girls had no idea what lay in store for them.

Once again, they were force-marched across the desert until reaching the Mohave encampment in a lush, fertile basin along the shores of the Colorado River, known today as Mohave Valley. If Olive knew where she was, she might have thought it ironic she had finally reached Bashan, the golden land James Brewster evoked in his teachings. She later recalled her first impression of the valley that spread before her:

We found the location and scenery of our new home much pleasanter than the one last occupied. The valley

extended about thirty or forty miles, northeast by south-
west, and varying from two to five miles in width.
Through its whole length flowed the beautiful Colorado,
in places a rapid, leaping stream, in others making its
way quietly, noiselessly over a deeper bed.

The Mohaves tended to be more compassionate than
their previous masters, but the girls were never allowed to
forget they were still prisoners. Nevertheless, the chief's
wife Aespaneo, and daughter Topeka, showed a semblance of friendliness by offering the girls blankets to
stave off chilling winds that blew across the swift-flowing
Colorado River.

Some time after settling in the Mohave village, Olive
and Mary Ann were decorated with indelible markings
that the Mohave people considered fashionable adorn-
ments. Each girl was subjected to numerous pricks along
her chin and arms, likely with a cactus spine, marking
deep lines in the skin.

Next, ground stone was mixed with the juice of a
weed and rubbed into the wounds, leaving permanent
tattoos. Some believed the Mohaves marked all their
slaves in this manner to identify them if they ran away.

However, the Mohaves applied these markings to themselves as well and considered them attractive embellishments.

The Mohaves relied on heavy winter rains to replenish the constantly flowing Colorado River. As the river overflowed its banks, it fed their crops of wheat and vegetables, providing an abundant food supply. Aespaneo and Topeka gave Olive and Mary Ann a plot of ground and a few seeds to grow their own crops, but Mary Ann remained weak and frail.

As the winter of 1855 blew in, it brought dry winds but little rain, parching the Mohaves' verdant fields. Before long, the entire village was on the brink of starvation. Olive, along with many of the villagers, traveled long distances searching for nuts, berries, seeds, anything to stave off hunger.

Sadly, Mary Ann was too weak to go on these hunts. Olive searched for birds' eggs to feed the little girl and often begged for morsels of food from anyone passing by. But nothing could save her little sister.

Even Olive could not recall exactly when her sister

died, but it was probably in the spring or summer after that winter that left so many villagers dead from starvation. The little girl was twelve years old and had spent her last four years on earth in captivity.

Now seventeen-year-old Olive was truly alone and no amount of solace from the sympathetic Mohaves could comfort her. Weeks went by before she finally accepted that she would live the rest of her life within the confines of this Indian village along the banks of the beautiful Colorado River.

She learned the Mohave language and took an interest in their religious beliefs, while teaching them what she could remember of her own faith. She dressed in Mohave fashion, which usually consisted of a bark skirt. She was still taunted and teased, but most of the villagers tolerated her presence and left her alone. Aespaneo and Topeka were her only friends. According to Olive, "Had it not been for her [Aespaneo], I must have perished."

In January 1856, word reached Fort Yuma (renamed from Camp Yuma) that two white girls had been seen in a Mohave village, but the army failed to send troops to investigate the rumor. Not until February, when a Quechan Indian named Francisco claimed he knew of a white woman living with the Mohaves, did the army agree to barter for Olive's release. At the time, no one was aware that Mary Ann had perished.

In exchange for one horse, Olive was turned over to Francisco and escorted to Fort Yuma. To ensure a safe return to her own people, the Mohave chief ordered his daughter Topeka and a small band of Indians to travel with Olive to the fort. Aespaneo sobbed as Olive left the Indian village.

As the group approached the fort, one of the Indians ran ahead and came back with a calico dress so Olive could return to her people properly clothed. She shed her bark skirt and donned the once-familiar garment.

On February 22, 1856, eighteen-year-old Olive Ann Oatman entered Fort Yuma, somewhat bewildered to be back among her own people after five long years of captivity.

Unknown to Olive, her brother Lorenzo, now nineteen years old, had survived the deadly attack on her family so many years ago. Battered and bloody, he had made his way back to Maricopa Wells. Never giving up the search for his sisters, Lorenzo was working in California when he received word of Olive's arrival in

Fort Yuma. It took him a month to make his way to the army camp, arriving on March 21, 1856. At first, the brother and sister stood silently staring at each other until both young people regained their tongues and were finally able to talk about their ordeals.

Over the ensuing years, Olive lectured across the country about her captivity. Reverend Royal Byron Stratton, who befriended the sister and brother shortly after Olive's release, wrote *Captivity of the Oatman Girls*, published in 1857, the first book about the massacre and the girls' imprisonment. It became an instant bestseller.

While speaking in New York in February 1864, Olive met Irataba, a Mohave chief, who was traveling with John Moss, a prospector and guide from Arizona. She asked the chief countless questions about the people she had known in the Indian village along the Colorado River. "Every stream and mountain peak and shaded glen I was as familiar with," Olive remembered, "as with the dooryard of my childhood home."

On November 9, 1865, Olive Ann Oatman married John Brant Fairchild and ceased lecturing. The couple eventually settled in Sherman, Texas, and adopted a baby girl. John Fairchild purchased every Stratton book he could lay his hands on (some did remain in the public domain), destroyed them, and ordered all who entered his home never to mention the nightmare Olive had endured for five long years. For the rest of her life, she bore the tattooed scars of her captivity on her chin and arms.

Olive died on March 21, 1903. She was finally reunited with the rest of the Oatman family.

CHILD OF HISTORY

Atanacia Santa Cruz (Hughes)
1850–1934

The years dissolved like rainwater trickling down the Santa Cruz River on a hot Arizona summer day. For over eighty years Atanacia Santa Cruz witnessed and contributed to the growth of the emerging Southwest, all the while journeying toward her own destiny in the desert community of Tucson. Through turmoil and transition, battles and business, not to mention true love, the girl with soft brown eyes and dark curly hair thrived along the banks of the Santa Cruz.

When Atanacia was born in 1850, only a handful of

houses stood on either side of an adobe-walled Mexican presidio that would evolve into the bustling town of Tucson. The small fortress, founded in 1775 in the name of Spain by Irishman Hugo O'Conor, was established along the banks of the Santa Cruz River to conquer marauding Apache Indians. In 1821, Mexico declared its independence from Spain and took over the presidio.

A war between Mexico and the United States (1846–1848) resulted in the Treaty of Guadalupe Hidalgo, which brought land into the United States that would eventually comprise parts of Arizona, California, New Mexico, Colorado, Nevada, and Utah. However, the treaty contained vague language regarding the boundaries between Mexico and the United States. Also, land necessary to build a railroad across the desert to California was not included in the agreement. Consequently in 1853, James Gadsden negotiated with Mexico to purchase thousands of acres that included territory south of the

Gila River to the present-day Mexican border. With the signing of the Gadsden Purchase Treaty in 1854, the southern part of Arizona came under U.S. authority.

Up until the time the United States took possession of this part of Arizona, Mexican military personnel and their families made up most of the presidio's population.

The presidio was an imposing structure with eighteen-inch-thick adobe walls towering ten to twelve feet high. In one corner, a watchtower pitted with countless portholes allowed sentries full view of the surrounding countryside, ever watchful for approaching Indians. The lone entrance, also heavily patrolled, consisted of an enormous mesquite wood gate that clanged shut with massive iron bars every night, or when danger lurked outside.

The Santa Cruz family lived in one of the first houses built outside the protective stockade.

Atanacia could not remember her father, Juan Maria Santa Cruz, who died of cholera the year after she was born. At the age of eight, she was orphaned when her mother, Manuela Bojorquez Santa Cruz, also died. The little girl went to live her sister Petra, six years her elder and already married to Hiram Stevens, one of the town's leading citizens. Atanacia and Petra remained very close all their lives, living a short distance from each other outside the walled presidio.

In March 1856, six-year-old Atanacia probably saw the last twenty-six Mexican soldiers ride out of town, the only protection the people of Tucson had against Indian attacks. Many living within the presidio followed the contingent back to Mexico, but the Santa Cruz family chose to remain in Tucson.

That November, Atanacia and her friends may have been playing hopscotch or ring-around-the-rosy in the center of town as troops of U.S. Dragoons rode in to oversee and protect the desert community against Indian invasions.

As Atanacia reached school age, she received little formal education. She learned what English she knew from visitors and townspeople, but it would not be until years later, sometime around 1880, when she took her first four children to Lawrence, Kansas, to attend school that she would conquer this "foreign" language. Her youngest daughter, Mary, born in 1886, remembered that her mother "wanted to talk in English and improve her vocabulary so she always spoke to me in English excepting when she was dissatisfied with conduct and so forth, why then she would always talk in Spanish."

During her childhood, Atanacia spent much of her time perfecting her sewing, and years later would become known for her intricate, beautifully patterned quilts.

Corpus Christi Day was special for the youngsters of Tucson. Although it was a solemn occasion, the day on which Christians commemorate The Last Supper of Jesus Christ and his apostles, Atanacia, along with other little girls, all dressed in pristine white frocks, marched like summer snowflakes through streets festooned with spring-green branches. They scampered under arches and arbors decorated with gauze and flowers of every color of the rainbow. The children were in awe of the brilliant colors and aromatic fragrances that permeated the town.

When Atanacia was a child, San Augustín Church, built in 1772, was already in a state of disrepair. The roof was falling in, unstable beams held up the ceiling, and debris covered the earthen floors. Although the arched double doors were barred to keep local children from playing among the ruins, most youthful trespassers had little trouble finding a way into the old house of worship.

One day, Atanacia and her friends discovered a name painted on one of the church walls, and they were soon scratching at the plaster and adobe to see what lay beneath the crumbling fragments. Before long they came across an old coffin, small enough for a baby. Clawing at the ancient partition, the girls continued to dig out the coffin until they managed to lift it from its resting place. Maybe sensing the ancient church would not last much longer, the children carried away the baby's coffin, dug a shallow grave, and reburied the abandoned infant. The long-forgotten child could now rest in eternal sleep.

Atanacia was seven years old when the first Butterfield Overland Stage Company from St. Louis to California came through town in 1857. According to the 1860 census, she was one of only 1,000 people living in Tucson, with less than 6,500 in the entire territory. Stagecoach travel brought a myriad of visitors to town. For about $200, a visitor could travel west in less than thirty days. Those headed eastward paid only $100. Meals provided at stage stops ran seventy-five cents to a dollar.

Among the travelers who arrived in Tucson was Samuel Hughes, a very ill young Welshman. Sam did not arrive by stage but staggered across the desert from California, a journey of unimaginable hardship. He may have been suffering from tuberculosis, and may also have injured his chest while lifting a deer carcass, both maladies leaving him gasping for breath. Whatever ills he was suffering left him stranded in the Old Pueblo as his companions continued on to Texas. He never left.

Sam spent his first night sleeping under the stars in a ditch outside the presidio. In those days, there were few places in town to bed down for the night. As one Tucson pilgrim noted, "[T]here is no tavern or other accommodations here for travelers, and I was obliged to roll myself in my blanket and sleep either in the street or the corral . . . " Old-timers described a Tucson bed as lying on one's stomach and covering that with one's back. Light was gleamed from the stars above.

Sam rallied from his ills and was soon thriving in the desert air. Although he had little education, he was a smart businessman and opened a butchering business selling meat and grain to the Butterfield Overland Stage Company, and later to the army.

Over the years, Sam Hughes played an integral role in establishing Tucson as a prosperous Southwestern city. He was one of the incorporators of the town as a municipality, served seven years as an alderman, became treasurer of Pima County as well as treasurer for the Territory of Arizona. He served a stint as Pima County sheriff, and for six years worked as the territory's Adjutant General. He was one of the organizers of the first Tucson bank as well as the Arizona Pioneers Historical Society.

Sam and Hiram Stevens, husband of Petra Santa Cruz, established a partnership that lasted many years. Sam surely ran into precocious little Atanacia when he visited Hiram, and it would not be long before the two formed a lasting bond.

During this time, Civil War broke out among the states, and tempers and tragedies kept communities and families separated and estranged for years. In February 1862, Confederate President Jefferson Davis declared Arizona Territory for the Confederacy. Within the month, eleven-year-old Atanacia curiously watched as Confederate troops marched into the desert town. Most people were happy to see the Southern soldiers arrive since the army once billeted there to protect the town against Indian attacks had been called back East to fight the war.

Sam Hughes was ordered to take the oath of the Confederacy or be shot. Since he fully supported the Union, he fled to California.

In May, Sam returned to Arizona, arriving behind a column of Union soldiers who rode into town just as the gray-clad Confederate troops departed. Atanacia watched stoically as the Confederate soldiers retreated before the overwhelming number of Union forces. Still a child, she was unsure what to expect from this show of military strength.

Sam Hughes also watched the Union contingent, but his eyes sought out the charming señorita he had not seen for several months. As he spied her among the throng that greeted the arriving troops, he realized Atanacia was growing into a beautiful young girl.

Sam wasted no time proposing to Atanacia, even though both of them lacked proficiency in a common language. Sam's native tongue was Welsh. He had conquered enough English to get by and knew a smattering of Spanish. With Spanish her native language, Atanacia probably had a hard time understanding Sam's broken

English. This may have hampered their conversation, but not enough to deter true love.

At first, she refused to marry him, claiming she would not make a good wife because she did not know how to cook or do the laundry. A descendant of one of the first families in Tucson—both her father and grandfather had been born inside the walled presidio—Atanacia was not obliged to perform daily household chores. She did know how to sew, however, and became one of the finest seamstresses in the territory. Sam assured her she would never have to cook or wash.

Pressing his proposal, Sam finally won the hand of young Atanacia. Just three months shy of her twelfth birthday, Atanacia Santa Cruz wed twenty-nine-year-old Sam Hughes on May 27, 1862, at the majestic Mission San Xavier del Bac, a few miles south of Tucson. The mission was originally named in 1700 by Father Eusebio Francisco Kino, a Jesuit missionary and one of the early Spanish explorers of the Southwestern desert.

With the early-morning dew still sparkling on the sparse grassland, Atanacia and Sam rode up to the hallowed mission, its stark white walls ascending from the brown desert floor, its stately spires reaching toward a

cloudless Arizona sky. They
stood awestruck before
the altar, behind which
a multitude of brilliant
colors were illuminated
by the rising sun.
Ancient paintings of saints
and mortals watched as they took
their vows.

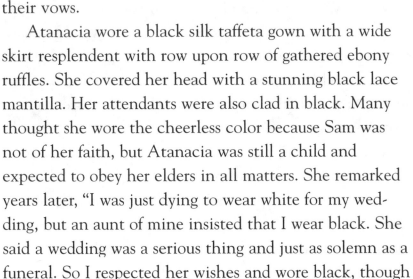

Atanacia wore a black silk taffeta gown with a wide
skirt resplendent with row upon row of gathered ebony
ruffles. She covered her head with a stunning black lace
mantilla. Her attendants were also clad in black. Many
thought she wore the cheerless color because Sam was
not of her faith, but Atanacia was still a child and
expected to obey her elders in all matters. She remarked
years later, "I was just dying to wear white for my wedding, but an aunt of mine insisted that I wear black. She
said a wedding was a serious thing and just as solemn as a
funeral. So I respected her wishes and wore black, though
I did not want to."

A large crowd gathered for the wedding and afternoon
reception at the home of friends living near the mission.

Returning to Tucson, Sam and Atanacia enjoyed another lavish wedding dinner at the home of Petra and Hiram Stevens. The newlyweds moved in with Atanacia's sister and husband, and deferred their honeymoon for a few years.

About a week after they were married, Sam told Atanacia to purchase whatever she needed, and plenty of it. She refused and recalled the ensuing conversation in her "Reminisces" recorded in the 1935 *Arizona Historical Review*.

> *You know, it was the custom in those days to lay in a big lot of cloth and keep a full trunk of things to make. I remember he said, "Get plenty to sew and get enough to pack away." But I had a trunk full already, at least I didn't want to buy any more just then, so I said, "I don't want anything." And he looked at me and asked, "Well, why don't you?" So I told him I didn't want to buy anything just then as I wanted our own home and would help him save money to get it. I said, "I want a home first, before I buy anything else."*

Sam left the house. When he returned that evening, he asked his new bride how she felt and, "he kept looking at me 'kinda' funny, so I thought there was something the matter with the way I looked." Presuming Sam was poking fun at her, she stormed, "What makes you keep asking me how I feel?" Sam laughed at the temper his young wife exhibited and then told her, "[Y]ou are in your own house now." He had bought the home from Hiram that day. The house Atanacia first lived in as an orphan after her mother's death would remain her home the rest of her life.

Situated on a large, grassy piece of land that would give the children who would be born to Atanacia and Sam plenty of room to romp and play, the house became a haven and meeting place for people from all walks of life. Sam held meetings to discuss the Indian situation with fellow townsmen. Atanacia, according to one of her granddaughters, ". . . was a great hostess. Her house was open to any of the dignitaries who came through town."

Through the years, Atanacia and Sam were an integral part of the growth of Tucson, lending their time and money to establish a viable community. One of their passionate projects involved promoting the foundation for a public school system that would benefit all of Tucson's children.

At age fourteen, Atanacia gave birth to her first child, Juan Baptist, but the baby did not survive. Nor did her second son, Theodore. But in 1865, still only a teenager, she gave birth to Isabel, a healthy baby girl. In all, Atanacia would bear fifteen children—five would not survive infancy.

Three years after they were married, Atanacia and Sam went on their long-awaited honeymoon. Baby Isabel accompanied them, as did Petra and Hiram Stevens.

The entourage started off in a new spring wagon sporting a white top, similar to the buggy that had taken the couple to Mission San Xavier del Bac on their wedding day. They headed south toward Arivaca, then Altar, and into Hermosillo, Mexico. A cook traveled with them and the touring party suffered few deprivations along the way.

In Hermosillo, they sent the cook and buggy back to Tucson, boarded a stagecoach for Guaymas where they caught a steamer for a seventeen-day ocean voyage up the coast.

On July 4, 1865, Atanacia and Sam landed in San Francisco. Having spent all her short life within the confines of Tucson's small desert community, Atanacia marveled at the huge stately buildings that lined the city streets, and found the throngs of people overwhelming. That evening, they enjoyed a bountiful display of fireworks in celebration of Independence Day. "I had never seen any [fireworks] before," she remembered. "And I think they were the nicest fireworks I have ever seen in my life."

For six weeks, the two couples enjoyed the sights, sounds, and smells that enveloped the busy seaport city. Sam bought Atanacia gold opera glasses so she could better view the actors at the theater. And Atanacia and Petra certainly must have browsed through the shops exclaiming over goods never seen in their desert hometown.

Before they left the big city, Sam bought Atanacia a Singer sewing machine, the first one ever brought to Tucson. "Whenever I would use it [the sewing machine]," said Atanacia, "people would gather around to watch me. They would also bring me all kinds of things to sew, and it did not matter to them whether I sewed with coarse or fine thread."

From San Francisco, the party traveled downstream to Santa Barbara, a small mission town. From there, they headed by stagecoach to Los Angeles where they remained until February 1868.

What a trip this must have been for Atanacia! She was still very young, but the sights she saw on this grand tour stayed with her the rest of her life.

In Los Angeles, Sam bought a pair of white horses and a new buggy for the return trip to Tucson. Thirty days after they left Los Angeles, they arrived back home. In her arms, Atanacia carried a baby girl, Margaret Frances, who had been born in Los Angeles in December 1867.

As the entourage returned to Tucson, unsettling events were happening in the Old Pueblo. Indian uprisings still occurred in the Southwest, leaving Tucsonans uneasy and fearful of venturing too far out of town. Atanacia refused to visit the two ranches she and Sam now owned. Only with an escort of soldiers would she go beyond the security of her home and neighborhood. She felt no guilt making bullets for the men who dared face roaming, marauding Indians who raided cattle and horses in the dead of night.

When townsmen attacked Indian villages, Indian captives were brought into town, including orphaned children. "[T]hey brought a lot of little ones into Tucson," Atanacia remembered. "These children were divided up among a number of us, but none of them lived long. They just drooped and got weak and died."

One had to be tough to survive in such an environment. Atanacia was tough and strong, but she was also a woman of grace and beauty. A granddaughter remembered her as "very precise, very beautifully dressed, very proper." However, "If you were naughty, she thumped you on the head with her thimble. But afterward she'd slip a lemon drop into your hand."

Atanacia Santa Cruz Hughes became a Tucson legend, surviving until 1934. Like the Santa Cruz River that still flows intermittently alongside the old Western town, she remains a constant reminder of a bygone era.

One of the artifacts she left for her children and future generations is an intricately sewn silk and satin quilt, a pineapple variation of a log cabin pattern. Housed at the Arizona Historical Society Museum in Tucson, the sharp black background of this beautiful quilt boldly

brings to life the still-brilliant blue, red, and gold embroidered floral motif that is commingled with religious symbols. In the center of the quilt, Atanacia stitched a golden key. Was it the key to her heart, the key to the city, or the key to the future?

DESERT ARTIST

Laurette Lovell (Francis)
1869–1936

Laurette limped toward the center of the room. After eighteen years, she could maneuver very well with her disproportionate legs. She had learned early on how to cope with her disability and it seldom deterred her from accomplishing anything she set out to achieve. As she made her way toward the imposing presence of General Nelson A. Miles, the man who had ended Indian uprisings in the Territory of Arizona in 1886, just one year ago, she walked cautiously, but proudly. She was about to present the General with one of her most unique and valued works of art, a gift of gratitude on behalf of the citizens of Arizona, and she prayed he would receive it as warmly as it was given.

Laurette Lovell had overcome almost as much strife and hardship as the General. Her triumphs did not resound across the nation, as did his undertakings; nevertheless, she had risen above her disability to accomplish much more than she dared dream, and she could certainly stand proud beside one of the most decorated military men in the country.

Laurette was born in San Jose, California, on January 31, 1869, with one leg four inches shorter than the other. Her parents, Judge William and Mildred Lovell, certainly took the youngest of their four children to numerous doctors, but none had a remedy that would even out the child's legs.

For many years, she wore a painful iron brace that was supposed to lengthen her shorter leg, but all it did was humiliate and embarrass her when she tried to keep up with her friends. She could not play hopscotch. She was too unsteady on her feet to play blindman's bluff. Even hide-and-seek left her exhausted. And puss-in-the-corner, where children run from corner to corner trying not to get caught, was completely beyond her capabilities.

She refused to wear a built-up shoe that would even her stride, maybe because she felt it made her deformity even more noticeable.

At an early age, Laurette discovered she liked to draw and paint, and her parents encouraged her to develop these talents through art classes, hoping that would keep her occupied since she couldn't ride, run, or even walk down the street without difficulty. When the Lovell family moved to Tucson in 1882, thirteen-year-old Laurette already excelled in a variety of artistic accomplishments. Once she surveyed the surroundings of her new home, she discovered that the desert held a new artistic medium to challenge her.

The town of Tucson lies next to the land of the Tohono O'odham people. The Tohono O'odham, or "Desert People," have lived in the arid Southwest for centuries, descendants of ancient Hohokam tribes that inhabited the Americas as far back as 400 to 500 B.C. From their ancestors, the Tohono

O'odham acquired a talent for farming and for creating *ollas* (oy-
yahs), or earthenware pottery.
These unglazed pots, usually
gourd-shaped with a wide
opening at the top, were made
from a variety of local clays. Once
hardened, with the solidity and stability
of the pot determined by the density of the heat, the
stoneware was used for carrying and storing water, seeds,
and grains, and as cooking utensils. When Laurette saw
these primitive containers, she realized she had found her
desert canvas.

She had already experimented with painting on a
variety of materials. Besides canvas, she embellished
porcelain and fine china, and even had a kiln of her own
for firing her artistic pieces. She experimented in oils,
watercolor, inks, and sepia, the dark brown pigment prepared from the secretion of cuttlefish. When Laurette
first picked up an *olla*, the teenager saw its surface as
another platform upon which to display the beauty of the
desert that she found so compelling.

Taking brush in hand, Laurette painted desert scenes

on these crude pots: ruins of old Spanish missions, Indian women and their children, fierce Apache raiders, and the legions of cactus with their spiky protuberances and colorful flowers that marched across the dry, parched landscape. Sometimes, she took photographs, then painted these images on the rough surface of the *ollas*.

Within a short time, her artwork on these simple containers became renowned, and she was lauded as one of the first Anglo artists to utilize Native American pottery as an art form. Quite possibly, she taught her talents to other Arizona artists, but none achieved the skill with their paintings as did young Laurette.

The petite, raven-haired girl, ringlets framing her porcelain features, became a socialite in the tiny hamlet of Tucson, not only because of her artistic creativity, but because she was a lively, energetic girl despite her misshapen legs. She embraced almost any activity the dusty town proffered. She rode horses (sidesaddle of course), occasionally took a turn in front of the lights of the theater, and relished masquerade balls. One newspaper article placed her at a paper ball with "Miss Lovell in elaborately printed paper dress."

Clad in the most fashionable attire of the day, she

may even have been a little vain about the fancy size four shoes she wore on her mismatched legs. The balls and dances were certainly exciting events for her, but her awkwardness on the dance floor must have left her devastated. She could never dance gracefully with a gentleman and had to stand with one foot turned outward to keep her balance as she mingled with party guests.

In 1887, Laurette was asked to produce one of her elaborately designed and now famous *ollas* as a gift for General Nelson A. Miles, the man who had negotiated the surrender of Geronimo, one of the most feared Apaches in the West.

After finding his mother, wife, and three children slain by Spanish troops in 1858, Geronimo had sworn vengeance against all whites. The Apache warrior wreaked terror and havoc upon white settlers until his surrender to General Miles on September 4, 1886. His imprisonment brought the majority of Native Americans under U.S. rule and governance.

"I was born on the prairies where the wind blew free and there was nothing to break the light of the sun," Geronimo once said. "I was born where there were no enclosures." After his capture, broken promises prevented him from returning to his Arizona homeland. In 1909, he died a prisoner on a reservation in Fort Sill, Oklahoma.

The man to whom Geronimo surrendered was no stranger to battle by the time he met up with the great Apache warrior. Nelson Appleton Miles had already distinguished himself in the Union Army during the Civil War before riding with forces that defeated Kiowa, Comanche, Southern Cheyenne, Lakota, and Nez Perce warring bands. After his defeat of Geronimo, he went on to fight in the Spanish-American War, and volunteered to serve during World War I, but his age kept him from attaining a commission.

Geronimo's surrender led to a gala celebration in Tucson in November 1887. Crowds waved flags and banners, shouted and cheered as General Miles paraded through town. People no longer had to dread marauding Indians stealing their cattle and horses, no longer had to watch with rifles loaded fearing an attack on their homes and families. They could now live free and safe.

On the evening of the celebration for General Miles, the Society of Arizona Pioneers held a gala ball with "dancing and literary exercises." The *Daily Star*, mentioning some of the gifts bestowed upon the General, described one presentation of "a floral sword wrought with deft hands from white roses, indicative of peace." However, the *Daily Star* called "the attraction of the evening" Laurette's presentation of the *olla* she had painted especially for the General.

The large *olla* carried multicolored scenes of the beautiful Mission San Xavier del Bac that lies just south of Tucson, a panorama of the prehistoric Casa Grande ruins, Indian women carrying burden baskets, a portrait of the ill-fated Geronimo, and numerous paintings depicting the rich, vibrant diversity of cactus and desert life.

The *Daily Star* recorded the meeting between the General and the talented teenager. "In this the proudest moment of my life," Laurette told the General as she handed him the elaborately decorated *olla*:

> *I have the honor to present you this small tribute of gratitude and esteem from one of the daughters of Arizona. The [scenes depicting] peaceful civilization shows you the blessings . . . we enjoy in times of peace which you have so signally helped to bring to our sun kissed land. The ruins of Casa Grande are the only tokens of Arizona's past greatness. The century plant is the symbol of our*

perennial strength. The cactus shows our long endurance of trials, thirst, and want. I now . . . present you this olla in the name of the daughters of Arizona for your noble and distinguished services in their behalf.

As General Miles took the pot from Laurette, he lauded the men who fought by his side, then praised Laurette for her portrayal of the Arizona desert and its people:

You appeal to my love of the beautiful and the beauty of your country and my appreciation of the picturesqueness of its aborigines and their history and former grandeur, as well as the traditions of your country. This olla will be a lasting pleasure to me and my family. Wherever we may go, it shall ever remind us of this fair land and its people who have shown me so much love. My knowledge of Arizona enables me to realize that you have pictured its scenes, its character, and you have added to it by your artistic skill, and have displayed its beauties in a way that will be cherished and lasting.

Accepting an invitation from General Miles and his

wife, Laurette visited the Miles family at their home in Washington, D.C., where she enjoyed the cream of Capitol Hill society. Laurette's granddaughter, Laurette Lovell Johnson, claimed her grandmother held her debutante ball in the nation's capital as a guest of General and Mrs. Miles, that her paintings once hung in the Capitol Building in Washington, D.C., and that she was commissioned to paint a portrait of General Miles by the U.S. Government. But it was her portrayal of the desert and her use of Native American pottery that brought the attractive artist fame.

In 1890, work began on the elaborate and massive World's Columbian Exposition to be held in Chicago, Illinois, in 1893. It was the first time women were allowed to participate in the organization of a national exposition, and the first time federal funds were used to build a Women's Pavilion in which to display a profusion of women's arts and crafts from around the world.

President Benjamin Harrison appointed a board of seven Lady Managers to run the programs for the Women's Pavilion. The youngest member he selected was the representative from the Territory of Arizona, Laurette Lovell. From 1890 until the Exposition opened on May 1, 1893, Laurette traveled across Arizona meeting with various social and business groups to discuss the importance of representing women's talents and abilities at the fair. She encouraged women of all races and cultures to show their arts and crafts at the Exposition.

Journeying to distant reservations, she persuaded Navajo women to display their colorful, intricately woven blankets, and convinced Apache women to submit their elaborate, decorative baskets. And of course, she wanted the *ollas* of the Tohono O'odham people to be part of the Arizona exhibit.

Young Laurette was also called upon to design the official seal for the Arizona exhibit at the Exposition.

The Women's Pavilion at the Chicago World's Fair attracted thousands of spectators who viewed the showcased works of multitudes of women from around the world. The profusion of displays within the Pavilion was an astounding success.

Daily, women gathered to discuss ideas on social, business, and political issues. As one woman reported, "If in a different age and under other governments women have been suppressed, at the Columbian Exposition at least they are guaranteed the right of free speech under the most favorable circumstances. Such a dissemination of thought cannot fail to broaden woman's sphere of usefulness and facilitate her advancement."

Women returned home with new thoughts and ideas about public affairs, and the country almost immediately saw an influx of women join the political arena. Suffrage leader Susan B. Anthony remarked that the Exposition did more for the women's movement than twenty-five years of agitating.

Even after the last of the fairgoers returned home, Laurette stayed on in Chicago until 1895 to ensure that all of the exhibits in the Women's Pavilion were returned to the states and countries of their origins. On her return trip to Tucson, she first went to California where she tarried awhile in Los Angeles after meeting the man who would become her husband.

On July 6, 1895 Laurette and Will Evelyn Francis married in Los Angeles. They made their first home among the gold fields of Acton, California, where Will had acquired substantial property. Their only child, Evelyne Laurette, was born on June 6, 1896, in a hotel room in Acton. Ten days after their daughter's birth, with most of the gold mines in the area on the brink of closing, the couple returned to Arizona. They spent six months in Phoenix before coming home to the desert of Tucson.

Laurette continued to paint the landscape of the desert on the *ollas* of the Tohono O'odham people, as well as in a multitude of paintings, until 1908 when she and her family moved to Los Angeles. Even then, she created designs on china, drawings for store newspaper ads and other commercial illustrations, plus elaborate wallpaper layouts.

Laurette Lovell Francis died on February 28, 1936, at the age of sixty-seven.

Today, only four of her beautiful clay *ollas* are known to exist: two in California, including the intricately painted vessel Laurette presented to General Miles; and two in Arizona, one at the Arizona Historical Society Museum in Tucson. Laurette's granddaughter, Laurette Lovell Johnson, also donated many of her grandmother's paintings, plus a hand-painted Havilland china cup and saucer, to the Arizona Historical Society Museum.

Laurette Lovell is renowned for her work with Indian pottery. Although pottery art itself was a popular medium during the late 1800s, no one but young Laurette decorated the crude *ollas* crafted by Native American people. She found a unique new canvas upon which to display her talents.

"Laurette Lovell was one of the first great painters of Western scenes," her granddaughter claimed. "While California claimed her by birth, her adopted state of Arizona had her love, for in Arizona she did her most prolific work and that for which she is best known."

MIXED BLOOD

Anna Magdalena Box (Neal)
1870–1950

The days and weeks seemed all jumbled together like one of Annie's wooden jigsaw puzzles. She had no idea how long they had been traveling this westward trek from Oklahoma to Arizona, but her feet assured her she had been walking for a mighty long time. Her eyes welled with tears every time she scanned the horizon for a glimpse of an approaching town or even a far-off ranch. The tears came not so much from distress but in response to the searing sun that penetrated her very soul and made her eyes overflow when she stared too long across the glaring wasteland for some sign of civilization.

She reached for the water bucket to relieve her sun-dried lips, then remembered the liquid supply was dangerously low. She thought she could hold out a little longer before taking a sip, providing she did not think too much about how delicious it would feel trickling down her parched throat. Water was the key to their survival, particularly in this inhospitable wilderness, and there was precious little of it left as nine-year-old Annie and her parents, along with the rest of the wagon train, made their way west in 1879.

Annie Box was born on the Cherokee Nation in Oklahoma Territory in 1870. The Cherokee people had lived and flourished in the South for many years, adopting many of the white man's customs, including owning black slaves. As a whole, however, the Cherokee treated their slaves with much more dignity and respect than did white slave owners, and often the two races intermarried.

When gold was discovered on Cherokee land in the early 1800s, the U.S. Government confined the Cherokee, and their slaves, to stockades. More than two thousand perished. Those who survived were force-marched over one thousand miles into Oklahoma Territory during the harsh winter of 1838–39, leaving one thousand five hundred dead along this "Trail of Tears."

Annie's mother, Hannah Box, possessed both Cherokee blood on her mother's side, and black heritage through her father. Hannah's ancestors probably walked and survived the horrific and devastating "Trail of Tears." According to Annie, her father Wiley Box was of English parentage on his paternal side, and his mother from New Orleans. Whether Wiley's mother was of black descent is uncertain.

Annie's mixed blood created a strikingly handsome young girl with creamy tan skin and liquid ebony eyes. She would grow to six feet tall and held herself as regally as the most noble of queens. Her father is believed to have called her his "Cherokee Princess." It was because of her father's health that the Box family decided to leave the Cherokee Nation and head west.

Wiley Box came down with yellow fever, a viral disease caused by a mosquito bite. His skin turned yellow and he shook with fever. Annie worried because he could not eat when his head started pounding and his stomach hurt so badly. Medical wisdom of the day prescribed the dry heat of the West to cure his fever, so Annie and her mother packed up their belongings, and the Box family joined a wagon train heading across the Oklahoma plains and deep into the unsettled, sweltering Arizona desert.

The journey took the group through dry, barren, hot valleys desperate for rain. Between the arid basins, they faced steep precipices that had to be climbed and conquered, hills so vertical no mules or oxen could drag a wagon filled with furnishings up and over the sheer inclines. Everything had to be unloaded. Heavy chests filled with clothing and precious, scant food supplies were hand-carried up the hills. Some had brought heirloom furniture (including weighty pianos), much of which lay abandoned at the bottom of each new elevation. Even small children were ousted from their wagons and forced to walk up the sheer, rock-encrusted slopes. Everyone, including Annie, carried something.

With chains and ropes lashed to the wagons, those

strong enough became beasts of burden themselves, hauling carriages to the top of an unforgiving peak. After
hours of backbreaking labor, the group finally reached the
top of a hill and sprawled exhausted, gasping for water.
But there was never enough to quench one's thirst after
such an ordeal. The promise of water kept Annie, and
the rest of the wagon train, moving forward to confront
and surmount the next rise.

When she scanned the horizon for any signs of life,
the one thing Annie did not want to see was a band of
Indians headed their way. And as hot, exhausted, and
dangerously thirsty as the campers were after climbing
steep bluffs all day with little respite, the cold dark nights
brought new terrors into their quarters. No fires were
allowed for fear the flames would call attention to their
presence on the desolate plain. Indians still roamed far
and wide, and they often threatened travelers who passed
over their land. Those who could handle a gun or rifle
stayed alert most of the night. Annie listened to the
howls of coyotes and other strange creatures as she cow-
ered beneath the blankets waiting for the warm morning
sun to melt away the terrors of darkness.

Annie Box was by no means the only child on the

wagon train. She had the company of many girls and boys who traipsed along the trail enjoying the greatest adventure of their young lives.

Initially, all the children, including Annie, reveled in the excitement of the journey, even if thirst and fear sometimes inhibited their spirits. They made games out of natural objects found along the trail including lizards, scorpions, and other animals they had never seen before. As Cathy Luchetti noted in her book, *Children of the West: Family Life on the Frontier*:

> *At the first sound of "Wagons ho!" children swung down from their passenger perches to walk alongside the covered wagons, feet scuffing the dust, eyes darting in search of any diversion—a bush, a bone, a bird, a stone—to distract them from the weary miles ahead. Trailside treasures could be anything from shiny green mesquite beans to a sparrow egg or an arrowhead, to use in a game of chance or competition. Even cow bladders had potential. When inflated, they bounced as high as a balloon.*

But some days, Annie just wished they had stayed in Oklahoma Territory and not started this long, arduous journey. Days and weeks passed until the dusty town of Tucson appeared through the sand and grit like a mirage on the far horizon. Annie was so happy to arrive at their destination that no matter what the town offered, she was determined to like it.

Once called a place where the wicked flourished and murder went unpunished, where dozens of saloons lined the streets, Tucson was slowly growing into a respectable community. By January 1880, train travel was just a few split rails away. Churches seemed to sprout up every few weeks, and the brand-new St. Mary's Hospital rose from the desert floor, a haven for the sick and weary.

Schools, however, were not progressing as rapidly, which probably suited Annie just fine. Already an expert rider, she preferred the outdoors where she could ride to her heart's content, her long, shiny black hair flying behind the strongest, most spirited horse she could find. Cooped up in a hot, stuffy schoolroom all day trying to learn to read and do sums was not to her liking.

The first public school in Tucson, established in 1867, had closed down within months due to lack of money, and few educational institutions had been established during the ensuing years.

More successful were the Sisters of Saint Joseph who founded the Sisters Convent and Academy for Females, a private school, in 1870.

That year a group of nuns from St. Louis, Missouri, made their way to Tucson to run the new school. The journey was a dreadful experience for the novice travelers. Going by way of San Francisco, the women sailed by steamer to San Diego and were seasick almost the entire trip. Enduring a horrendous ride over uneven, rutted roads from San Diego into Yuma, the sisters almost drowned crossing the Colorado River where they then encountered the harsh desert. Coyotes and snakes invaded their tents and their nightmares. "It is beyond description," said Sister Monica, one of the nuns on this terrible trip, "what we suffered in riding two hundred miles in country like this."

Yet the town of Tucson came out tenfold to welcome the weary voyagers with church bells echoing across the desert, a grand parade through the center of town, fireworks, and a magnificent feast. By the time Annie arrived in Tucson nine years later, the Sisters Convent and Academy for Females was firmly established.

When the Box family entered Tucson, they were

identified as African-American despite their Cherokee and white bloodlines. The 1880 census lists only 155 African-Americans in Arizona Territory, most of them former Buffalo Soldiers who had retired from the 9th and 10th Calvary out of nearby Fort Huachuca. Apache Indians supposedly bestowed the "Buffalo Soldier" nickname on black troops who had served in the military since 1866.

With Indian raids still a force to reckon with, townspeople were more concerned with the local Indian population than the small number of African-American faces that appeared in town. The Boxes quickly became part of the community and enrolled their daughter in the Sisters Convent and Academy for Females.

Shortly after placing Annie in school, Wiley and Hannah Box headed out across Arizona Territory to prospect for gold, and they did locate and stake a few claims containing miscellaneous ores. Gold had been found along the Colorado River just north of the town of Ehrenberg in 1862. Within months, prospectors recorded successes in other regions, and the interest in desert gold had not ceased in the ensuing twenty years. The Boxes wanted their share.

Annie may have wished to go with her parents into the wilds of Arizona, but she soon came to value the education she received at the hands of the Sisters of Saint Joseph. She loved wandering through the flowering gardens that surrounded the school. She studiously learned French under the tutelage of Sister Eu Frazeer, worked in the school kitchen with Sister Cabello (which would come in handy later on), and played the piano during Sister Clara's music class.

Annie's musical talents flourished so much that she also took lessons in town from Mrs. Jacob Mansfeld, wife of the owner of Arizona's first bookstore. Along with teaching her the refinements of the piano, Eva Mansfeld encouraged Annie to pursue her flair for writing music.

Although history records that, with the help of Mrs. Mansfeld, Annie had two of her musical scores published very early on, neither piece can be found today. And only one titled score can be identified. Annie composed "Oklahoma March," maybe as a

remembrance of her trek across the dry, desolate, frightening plains and up and across all those unforgettable hills only a few short years before.

Annie's school years were brief. At the age of fourteen her health deteriorated and she could not keep up with her studies. She left school and traveled with her parents while they searched for their pot of gold. Apparently, traipsing across desert breathing the clear, dry, pristine air worked miracles on Annie's constitution. Within the year, she was back riding horses, the faster the better.

As soon as she was old enough to attend dances in town, Annie took to them like one of her wild steeds. She was often seen on the arm of one of the soldiers stationed at Fort Lowell twirling around the dance floor at Carillo Gardens, an amusement park with copious shade trees, flowering rosebushes, even a crystal-clear, man-made lagoon.

Carillo Gardens was the social center of Tucson and Annie danced polkas, waltzes, square dances, and quadrilles throughout the warm summer evenings. The color of her skin seemed of no consequence to her amorous escorts.

Annie's sister Josephine, eighteen years younger, acknowledged that her big sister "was lively, high spirited and a born flirt." Josephine also described Annie as "a beautiful girl. She grew tall and straight as a saguaro. Her dark beauty and her light step clearly showed her Indian ancestry."

According to author Barbara Marriott, Annie soon married one of her dance partners, soldier James Lewis, around 1884 or 1885. Lewis was assigned to Fort Yuma and the couple headed off for their new home along the shores of the Colorado River.

In 1885, Hannah and Wiley Box were arrested for robbing a man of $1,000. Although they were found innocent at their trial, their erratic and nomadic lifestyle could have been the impetus that led Annie to marry so young. She may have been seeking a more settled existence, a home and family of her own.

Annie's marriage to James Lewis was brief. She married again in 1887 to William Easton, but this marriage also ended in failure.

Love finally found Annie in 1892 when she married

William "Curly" Neal, twenty years her senior.

Curly was also a product of the Cherokee Nation with his family a mixture of Cherokee, African-American, and Caucasian. After scouting for William Frederick "Buffalo Bill" Cody in the 1860s, Curly joined the U.S. Army until arriving in Tucson the year before the Boxes came to town. At the time he and Annie married, Curly was running a lucrative business hauling freight and mail to and from the mines around Oracle, Arizona, a small ranching community about forty miles north of Tucson. Noted author Richard Harris in his book, *The First 100 Years: A History of Arizona Blacks*, contends that in the late 1800s, Curly Neal was considered the wealthiest African-American in Tucson.

When Hannah Box died in 1894, Annie was completely devastated by the loss of her mother. She and Curly had been married only a couple of years and he tried his best to roust his wife from her depression, but nothing seemed to work. Finally, he decided the best thing for her was a diversion.

Within a few months, Annie found herself deep in the throes of building and furnishing a new hotel in the mining settlement of Oracle, nestled in the bosom of the

Santa Catalina Mountains. The Mountain View Hotel became not only the showplace of Oracle, but renowned throughout the country. For $2.50 a day or $12.50 a week, people enjoyed the cool mountain breezes; the magnificent two-story, twelve-room hotel; and Annie's fine cooking.

The *Los Angeles Herald* gushed over Annie's graciousness, lauding her as "one of the most charming, genial and appreciative of landladies, who understands how to perform the difficult art of providing the best accommodations including a bill of fare, so as to make all feel pleased, at home and perfectly at ease."

She also looked after the health and well-being of her clientele. Physicians sent their tuberculosis patients to the Mountain View, knowing that between the clean, dry mountain air and Annie's good cooking, they would recover from their debilitating illness.

She started a school for her patrons' children, baptized the newborn babies of Oracle with the blessings of the Catholic Church, and could outshoot practically any man. The one exception, she claimed, was her husband's old scouting partner, "Buffalo Bill" Cody, who owned property in the area and often stayed at the Mountain

View. Annie said Cody was "the only hotel guest to whom I ever lost a shooting match." She was content with her life.

As soon as Arizona gained statehood in 1912, however, factions rode in that changed and influenced the lives of African-Americans across the state, including Annie and Curly Neal. Shortly after the Tucson school board refused to fund a school for African-American students, the Ku Klux Klan arrived in town.

Over the years, Annie and Curly watched as the people of Oracle turned away from them. They were no longer invited to gatherings, no longer hailed when neighbors passed by. Only when money was needed for a cause were they acknowledged. The bias and intolerance of racism had caught up with them in the tiny hamlet of Oracle.

The long waiting list for a room at the Mountain View Hotel dried up and the magnificent lodge fell into disrepair. The fireplaces stood cold and uninviting, while the balconies surrounding the hotel remained littered with oak leaves and desert dust.

In a 1948 interview with *The Magazine Tucson,* Annie, now widowed, sat with a Long Tom rifle across her lap and fondly remembered the guests who "came from all over and we had gay times, despite the simplicity of our pleasures."

Mrs. Neal still makes her home here, surrounded by mementoes of her colorful past, sitting quietly in her wheel chair as she relives in memory the long gone days when bloodthirsty Apaches lurked behind the boulders of Perfect Box Canyon and renegade white bandits created in reality what is now the glamorous legend of the Old West.

Annie Magdalena Box Neal died in 1950 at the age of eighty. The little girl who was a mixture of races and cultures is remembered as a tall, soft-spoken woman who cared deeply for the people around her regardless of the color of their skin.

PANDORA RANCHER

Edith Olive Stratton (Kitt)
1878–1968

Heavy rains had fallen in the mountains all week when
Edith Stratton crossed the San Pedro River to fetch the
mail. Her parents were always eager to see what the stage
brought in, and she was more than happy to jump on her
horse and tear across the dry riverbed to the stage stop.
The waterway contained nothing but rocks and deep, dry
silt that her horse Little Bill kicked up, coating the child
in a downy layer of silvery dust. Her two dogs, scuffling
along the bone-dry path, were also covered in the soft
sediment and could have passed for spooky gray wolves.

After retrieving the mail, she headed home. Suddenly, a terrifying roar enveloped the entire valley—overflow from torrential rains of the last few days came careening down the mountains, approaching with deadly force. Within minutes, the San Pedro would fill and flood with wave upon wave of raging water thrashing at the restrictive shoreline.

Edith thought she could outrun the oncoming torrent and urged Little Bill toward the water's edge. Just as she reached the embankment, a towering wall of water spilled down the dry riverbed obliterating everything in its path.

Uprooted trees zigzagged and bounced from one bank to the other, ramshackle buildings tumbled along like small pebbles in the wake of the oncoming deluge, even unsuspecting animals were at the mercy of the churning, muddy rapids.

Still determined to reach the safety of home on the other side of the river, Edith urged Little Bill into the swiftly rising waters. The horse obeyed and almost instantly, the angry river engulfed him. Losing his footing, he reared on his hind legs and turned sharply back toward shore. Riding without a saddle, Edith clung to the panicked horse, but his quick turn sent her plummeting into the deadly current. She fought her way back to the mud-slick riverbank and climbed ashore just ahead of Little Bill.

Her dogs had been smart enough to stay put and watch the terrifying scene unfold before them.

Above the thundering waters, she heard her mother calling from the other side of the river. Shouting above the roaring rapids, Edith answered she was safe and would stay put for the night and see how swollen the river looked in the morning. She shed her sopping-wet clothes and spread them out to dry. "It was very hot and there was no danger of catching cold," she remembered. As the long, lonely night wore on, however, she was not sure she had made the right decision to wait on the riverbank. Years later, she wrote of her ordeal, and of her time on the Pandora Ranch, in a book she authored with her father, *Pioneering in Arizona: The Reminiscences of Emerson Oliver Stratton and Edith Stratton Kitt:*

The coyotes seemed very near, but the dogs silenced them by their barking. I slept fitfully until a low growl from the dogs started me to an upright position. There,

not fifteen feet away, meandered a most beautiful
skunk. Why I ran and jumped on my horse I cannot
tell, but I soon got control of myself and helped the dogs
to drive the skunk off into the brush. At daylight I
dressed and went down to the river. It was just a trick-
ling little stream, and there on the other side was Mother
coming to meet me.

Far from her first or last encounter with nature, Edith
Stratton thrived on each new adventure she encountered
on the family's Pandora Ranch in the wilds of the Santa
Catalina Mountains in southern Arizona. Even the day of
her birth gave insight that her life would be anything but
ordinary.

Edith was in a hurry to be born on December 15,
1878. Her mother, Carrie Stratton, a New England
woman of refinement, sent her husband off to fetch the
doctor. Emerson Stratton scoured the central Arizona
town of Florence until he finally found the inebriated
physician playing cards in the back room of a saloon.
Fortunately, little Edith arrived safe and sound without
the doctor's attendance.

At the time of Edith's birth, the Stratton family—

mother, father, and sister Mabel who was six years older than the new arrival—lived in a dirt house in Florence, a halfway station on the stage route from Casa Grande to the Silver King mine near present-day Superior. The earthen floor of their house dropped eight inches below ground, and the dirt walls were protected by a cloth ceiling, which worked fine in Arizona's temperate climate until it rained. A soft, gentle sprinkling evoked no problems, but when a storm blew in, water dripped through the cloth ceiling until it eventually caved, spewing water over everything in the house and turning the floor into a sea of mud.

Occasionally, a local bar, the only building in town with a wooden floor, was cleared of besotted cowboys so townspeople could enjoy a community dance. One evening, Carrie Stratton placed baby Edith on one of the long benches before joining her husband on the dance floor. Glancing over as she twirled around the saloon, Carrie was shocked to see a man approach and start to sit on her little girl. That was the last time Carrie, or Edith, went to the dances.

When Edith was eighteen months old, Emerson Stratton moved his family from the little dirt house in

Florence to an even rougher existence in the Santa
Catalina Mountains to try his hand at ranching.
According to Edith, the family lived in "a dugout, a
dwelling actually dug out of the side of a hill. It had three
walls of 'mountain,' a dirt floor and roof, and a real door
and windows which Dad had brought with him from
Florence." Eventually, Emerson built a proper house for
his growing family.

With scant money coming in, Emerson Stratton
called his ranch Pandora after the Greek myth about a
box that spilled out all the ills of the world, leaving only
hope inside.

That first year on the ranch found the rattlesnake
population outnumbering the Stratton family. After
Emerson killed fifty of the slithering varmints, Carrie tied
two-year-old Edith to a bedpost to keep her from getting
out of the house unattended.

"I guess I could always ride," she recalled in her mem-
oir. Before she could even sit up, her father carried her on
his horse around Florence "in a sling made of an old
tablecloth knotted around his neck and shoulder, forming
a hammock. By the time we moved out to the ranch,
however, I was riding on a pillow in front of him. I can

remember the day I graduated from that and he let me ride behind. It was very thrilling, but I held onto his shirt like a leech."

An enterprising child, she made toys from strings of buttons and spools of thread, pieces of brightly colored glass from broken bottles, even beans. She experimented with scissors by cutting the fringe off a shawl and the hair off one of the dogs before chopping off her own tresses. Edith and sister Mabel played "ranch," like other little girls played house. Horses were crafted from stalks of beargrass with bushy, flowery tails. Cattle consisted of round yucca fruit for bodies and sticks for legs. Living on a working ranch, the girls also butchered their yucca-fruit cattle and prepared pretend beef jerky.

Next to the creek, the two little ranchers planted barley. If it actually sprouted, either the real cattle ate it, or the creek overflowed and washed their garden away.

On hot summer days, Carrie Stratton bathed her girls

down by the creek in waters caught in a depressed rock. "Once we took to 'sea' in Mother's wash tub, but got shipwrecked and had to go to bed while our clothes dried."

Dolls held no interest for the little cowgirl. "Once I was given a cloth doll with a china head, but she did not last long. I took her down to the corral to watch the cowboys brand calves, and she got excited and fell off the fence and broke her head."

Her one true friend was the imaginary Diggie. "She was my constant companion for many years. Sometimes she was just a stick, sometimes a handkerchief with a stone tied on one corner for a head; but most often she was . . . 'just there.' I could always talk to her and tell her all my troubles, and she was a great comfort."

Eventually, there would be four Stratton children—Mabel, Edith, Johnny, and Elmer—and all shared rides on the faithful steed Little Bill. "We usually rode bareback because we could get more of us on that way. First I would cup my hands and form a stirrup to help Mabel up. Then between us we could boost the two boys on. The trick was to get me on without pulling the boys off."

Edith and Little Bill often rode out to bring in

wandering range cows. "Once we were driving a cow along a fence when she suddenly turned back. Little Bill turned as suddenly as she did—but I kept going." Although she fell off many horses while growing up, none ever wandered off leaving her stranded.

Ten-year-old Edith learned to shoot after her grandfather presented her with a single-barrel, sixteen-gauge shotgun. Ammunition, however, was in short supply, for shells were an expensive purchase. She waited hours to get a bead on several birds at once before firing to preserve the little ammunition she had.

Once I shot three teal duck swimming in a row . . . I wounded them all, and after thinking that I had successfully wrung their necks I packed them home behind me. When Mother asked me what I was holding behind me, I proudly threw them down in front. One lay still, one ran under the house, and the third started to flutter off but the dog caught it. Mother stuffed all three with onions and we had roast duck for supper.

Skunks abounded around the ranch house, "squealing and knocking against the floor at night." One year, Edith set traps and made fifteen dollars selling skunk skins for fifty cents to a dollar apiece.

Fetching water uphill from the creek and tending to sooty coal-oil lamps were part of Edith's daily chores. Milking cows meant dodging unexpected kicks by an indignant beast, and Edith often tied the cow's legs together before starting her milking duties.

Riding bucking calves was great sport. Climbing onto the cow backwards and locking her feet under its neck, Edith lay prone across the calf's back and clung to its flanks. Sometimes suffering a bloody nose if the calf abruptly bolted, she did "not recommend this way of riding and can guarantee you will not stay on long."

Carrie Stratton disapproved of her children associating with rowdy cowboys and never adapted to the wildness of the West. Edith strained against her mother's rules and regulations, and she often regretted all she missed "by not being a cowboy among cowboys."

However, cowboys taught Edith how to make lassos by scraping the flesh from stretched, wet cowhide. "The cutting of long narrow strips by going around and around the

hide, the straightening of the strips by soaking and stretching, and then the braiding into a *reata* was quite an art."

They also taught her how to twist horsehair into rope using a *tarabilla*, a notched stick that twirled around and around, twisting the horsehair into a taut strand. "Once I let go of a strand, and it jumped and twisted and knotted up so that the man was not able to straighten it. That ended my twisting for some time to come."

One day, she and a ranch hand herded horses up a mountain. Looking across the splendor of the San Pedro Valley, the cowboy almost whispered, "I don't see how anyone could help but believe in God."

"I was only a small girl," said Edith, "but I have never forgotten his words. I think they added something good to my life."

She excelled on a horse and became a first-rate shooter, but young Edith had little talent in the kitchen. Standing on a box beside her mother, she struggled to roll out bread dough. "My piece was small, and after I had dropped it on the floor a couple of times you could not tell whether it was white bread or spice cake."

While life on the ranch was harsh at times, Edith and her siblings never felt deprived, especially when it came to sweets. Wild bees lived in hollow oak trees that surrounded the property. "The trick was to find them," she said.

The children attracted the bees by strategically putting out saucers of sweetened water. When a bee lingered at the water, they sprinkled it with flour so they could follow its trail to the hive. Once they located the hive, the children allowed ranch hands to perform the tricky business of getting the honey out. Carrie Stratton made jams and jellies from the sweet nectar, adding grapes and mulberries that grew wild along the creek bed.

All the children knew where Mother kept her sack of sugar and were often caught snitching a lump or five. If chores were completed on time, or a child was particularly good that day, Carrie Stratton rewarded with lumps of sugar flavored with wintergreen. The gang of four quickly learned to pool their sugar supplies and beg for a delicious batch of candy everyone could enjoy.

When provisions ran low, the family piled into the buckboard and headed toward Tucson, a two- to three-day journey. It was thirty miles to Tucson "as the crow flies," according to Edith, "but seventy-five miles as the road crawled."

Evenings spent on the trail brought visions of hissing snakes and howling coyotes into Edith's dreams:

Many a night the blood has absolutely congealed in my veins at the near and unexpected howl of a coyote which would be answered first from one hill and then from another until it seemed as if the souls of the dead were moaning and wailing and closing in on me. I would lie and sob to myself, but did not dare to cry out because I feared Dad's scolding worse than the coyotes. But at the end of the second day, as Mother hunted candles and nightgowns and took the clothes from our tired little bodies, we children would all cry together.

Indian scares were infrequent but also sent the family fleeing toward the safety of Tucson. To Edith, "[e]very barrel cactus was a crouching Apache and every bright star just tipping the distant Galiuros [mountains] was a signal fire."

The education of the Stratton children was not neglected just because they lived far from town. Tutors came and went on the Pandora Ranch until Carrie Stratton moved her children into Tucson during the winter months so they could acquire a proper education.

Bursting into the house after her first day of school, Edith raved to her mother about the new song she had learned called "Columbia the Jam in the *Olla*." *Ollas* were earthenware jars used by American Indians to carry beans, seeds, and water. Covered in burlap, these multi-faceted jugs kept water cool throughout the day.

The children had plenty of playmates during their months in Tucson, and warm evenings brought everyone outside. The game snap-the-whip usually found little Edith on the tail end where she would eventually end up flat on her face. Bushes growing right in the street gave the children plenty of secret places to play hide-and-seek.

Life in the Southwest grew even harder for the Stratton family when drought and overgrazed range grass meant less food for the Pandora cattle. The family eventually had to abandon the ranch after Emerson Stratton lost half his herd. In 1895, they moved back to Florence where Edith had been born seventeen years before.

Leaving the ranch was hard on all the children, but particularly for Edith. She had learned how to ride and shoot there; had sailed off toward the unknown in her mother's washtub; chased skunks, quail, and duck; and had survived the raging San Pedro River.

Edith finished her elementary education in Florence, then attended Los Angeles Normal School. As soon as she graduated, she headed back to the desert to teach. Whenever she found time, she took classes at the University of Arizona, but it took her twenty years to graduate. "I guess I was in school longer than anyone in the history of university," she once remarked.

In 1903, Edith married George Farwell Kitt, a native of England, and bore two children.

In 1925, she was hired as secretary for the Arizona Pioneers' Historical Society, formed in 1865 "to preserve the relics and paint the wonders of the past."

"That title 'secretary' was erroneous," she said, "for I had to be not only the corresponding secretary but also the librarian, researcher, entertainer, welfare worker, and father confessor all in one."

Under Edith's guidance and diligence, the organization, renamed the Arizona Historical Society, received numerous collections that eventually made it one of the finest research centers on Southwestern history.

Even after retiring in 1947, she continued to work on various research projects for many years.

Edith Stratton Kitt "was the historical society," said her friends. "She did more than any other single Arizonan to preserve, collect, and restore Arizoniana."

In 1966, when she was seventy-four years old, Edith moved to California to be near her daughter. She died two years later.

The little girl with the vivid imagination and driving ambition, who rowed a washtub on a grand adventure and stared down uncontrollable river waters, left her mark on Arizona by preserving the history of the state, and by leaving her own recollections of the remarkable years she spent on the Pandora Ranch.

THE RIDE OF HER LIFE

Mildred Back (Fain)
1879–1967

The wind felt cool on her skin as Millie Back and Tony, her gray pony, rode along Beaver Creek. Autumn was coming to central Arizona, although the sun would show no mercy later in the day as Millie made her way north to Oak Creek. She almost felt guilty not tending to her siblings for a whole day, or washing and ironing the stacks of clothing seven children accumulated. Today, she did not have to pick the ripened orchard fruit or gather end-of-the-season vegetables from the family garden. Her solo ride left her free as the wind that tousled her hair in the quickening breeze.

She slowed Tony's gait as she wandered along the creek bed, maybe to savor her liberty just a little longer.

She saw the men camped along the creek before she heard their voices. As they watched her approach, one of the men rose from the campfire and walked toward the little girl and her pony.

Tony sniffed the air and shook his head as if to ward off a foreboding scent. Millie also sensed something amiss, yet saw nothing but the approaching bearded cowboy, now only a few feet away.

Suddenly she jerked Tony's reins and sped toward the mesa above the men's campsite. Nothing but her keen instinct told the girl, not yet in her teens, that the campers were up to no good and she should put as much distance as possible between her and the strangers. Her intuition probably kept Millie from losing her life that day. With certainty, she would have been forced to forfeit the treasure hidden deep in the pocket of her skirt.

Keeping a sharp eye behind, she held tight to Tony's reins as the little horse dashed across the mesa. She was on a mission and determined to complete the most important task of her young life.

But oh, how she longed to be home caring for those sometimes-exasperating little brothers and sisters.

Marjorie Ann and William Beriman Back welcomed their firstborn child on September 17, 1879. At the time of Mildred's birth, the Backs were ranching along Oak Creek in Arizona's lush Verde Valley.

As soon as she was old enough, Mildred—or Millie as she was known—became the caretaker of her younger siblings who began arriving in rapid succession. With her mother relying on her oldest child to care for the babies, Millie chased after wandering toddlers, wiped their noses and their bottoms, fed, cleaned, and tended to their needs, cares, and demands.

When Marjorie Ann gave birth to twins Jennifer and Jessie in 1889, however, ten-year-old Millie packed her bag and headed out the door. As she lugged her big satchel outside, her father asked where she was headed. Millie, already caring for eight-year-old Fred, six-year-old Bertha, and little three-year-old Harry, angrily replied, "Well, it's bad enough to take care of kids when they come one at a time, but when they start coming two at a time, I'm leaving!"

By this time, the family had relocated from their Oak Creek property to the spacious Montezuma Well ranch that Bill Back had purchased for the price of two horses. The ranch lay about fifty miles south of the town of Flagstaff and derived its name from a natural spring that exists on the land, a watering hole that dates back millions of years.

Scientists believe an ancient cavern collapsed and formed this limestone sinkhole that contains high concentrations of carbon dioxide and alkali, preventing fish from living in the spring. However leeches, water scorpions, and turtles abound.

Soldiers who first saw the spring assumed that fifteenth century Aztec ruler Montezuma had ridden this far north, maybe even settled in the area since nearby cliff dwellings had also been named for the powerful warrior. But Montezuma never ventured into central Arizona, and both Montezuma Well and nearby Montezuma's Castle remain misnamed to this day.

Sitting 100 feet below the desert floor, the well spans about 470 feet across and descends to a depth of around 50 feet. Millions of gallons of water a day flow through the basin, with the water retaining a constant temperature of seventy-six degrees. A nearby cave contains a small pool the Back children called "Montezuma's Bathtub."

Prehistoric Hohokam and Sinaguan Indians used the spring to irrigate crops of corn, beans, and squash. Even as late as the 1800s, Western Apaches relied on the ancient waters to nourish their gardens until they were driven out by encroaching white settlements.

Neighbors thought Bill Back got a raw deal for his two horses. The Montezuma Well land was covered by an immense woodland of mesquite and tangled cat's claw vines, no place to raise cattle or any type of produce. But after clearing the land, the Back family put up enough fragrant mesquite firewood to keep them warm for several winters, and the orchard and gardens Bill planted generated abundant crops of luscious fruits and succulent vegetables.

The Backs ran pigs, sheep, cattle, and a few horses on the land, using a brand shaped like a Stetson hat. Bill Back set up his blacksmith shop in an ancient cave on the property, while his pigsty was built into another grotto. He also maintained a smokehouse, relying on Millie and the other children to stoke the fires that cured

the hams and bacon he sold
in Flagstaff.

Along with market-
ing hay and grain to
neighboring ranchers,
the Backs also sold the
produce from their large
orchard and prolific garden to
Flagstaff lumberjacks and railroad workers. Marjorie Back,
with the help of young Millie, supplemented the family
income by canning and selling the orchard's bounty. So
many people came and went at the Montezuma Well
ranch that in 1892, it became the logical place to establish a post office.

But if the crops failed, which they did one summer,
the entire family moved off the ranch and found work in
Flagstaff until the next rainy season afforded a more
lucrative crop.

Millie's first school years were spent at a small school-
house bordering Oak Creek. It was too far to walk, so she
hitched a ride to school on the back of one of her uncles'
horses. After the family moved to the Montezuma Well
ranch, however, she walked two-and-a-half miles each

way to the Beaver Creek school, keeping a sharp eye for Indians as she traveled the lonely stretch of road, even though Indian uprisings were now infrequent.

Millie may have been too young to remember the day at Oak Creek when an anticipated Indian attack sent everyone scrambling into wagons and dashing twelve miles south to Camp Verde and the safety of the military. She became well acquainted with the fort as she grew older, for she was often sent to the stronghold to bring back supplies.

The Montezuma Well ranch was not immune from an occasional Indian invasion, however. One morning, after Millie's father had left for the day, Marjorie Back was busily preparing breakfast for her children when a band of at least a dozen Indians boldly walked into the kitchen and started taking food right from under the startled children's noses. The stoic food snatchers then proceeded to scour the kitchen for any other groceries they could find, and took off laden with as much grain and corn as they could carry. Marjorie and

the wide-eyed children almost certainly let out a collec-
tive sigh of relief that no one was harmed during the
kitchen foray.

But Indians were not
Millie's problem that fateful
day in late September or
early October when she encountered the men camped along Beaver Creek.

Cattle ranchers in the Verde Valley drove their herds
into Flagstaff for sale and shipment. Traditionally, the
ranchers delegated one of their neighbors to collect the
sale proceeds and deliver the money to other ranchers.
This year, Frank Dickinson, Millie's uncle, was entrusted
with bringing the earnings of his neighbors back from
Flagstaff to Oak Creek. As he made his way along the
trail, he suddenly became very ill.

Stopping at his sister's Montezuma Well ranch house,
Frank languished for days unable to complete his journey.
Knowing his neighbors were waiting for their cattle
money to lay in stores for the coming winter, and with all
hands at the Back ranch busy with the fall harvest, no
one was free to make the fifteen-mile trip to pay off the
ranchers. Little Millie was the only child old enough, and

responsible enough, to be trusted with such a crucial and urgent errand.

A morning dew spread across the yard as Millie tightened Tony's saddle. Nothing could erase the grin that spread across her face. For a few days, she would be free from the burden of caring for her younger siblings, a chore she readily accepted but was glad to relinquish even for a short time. She also did not mind missing the last days of harvest before winter arrived.

As she settled onto the little pony, she reached down to ensure her precious cargo was secure. Pinned inside the pocket of her skirt, Millie felt the little purse that contained $5,000, the cattle money that belonged to Uncle Frank's neighbors. Patting the paper on which Frank had written instructions as to how the money was to be distributed, she made sure it was also tucked securely in her pocket.

A group of worried adults watched as horse and rider set off on a journey rife with danger. But Millie gaily waved as she and Tony fled the confines of house and ranch work. All went well until she encountered the men camping along Beaver Creek.

Millie had no idea whether the strangers were good or

evil, but as she started across the mesa and heard their crude remarks and raucous laughter, she knew she was in harm's way. How right she was!

Not until later did Millie learn that the strangers along the creek were wanted horse rustlers with a deputy sheriff hot on their trail. They were captured over seventy miles away near Cave Creek after a fierce gun battle that left at least one of the outlaws dead.

A little wiser and a lot more cautious, Millie rode on to Oak Creek and delivered the money to the ranchers without further incident. She hastened back to the Montezuma Well ranch and into the arms of her relieved parents and clamoring siblings.

When her father turned the ancient Montezuma Well into a tourist attraction, Millie, along with the other children old enough to help, stood before the watering hole and charged visitors fifty cents for a guided tour. For an additional twenty-five cents, Bill rowed the sightseers out onto the waters of the limestone lake.

Scouring the area for pieces of old pottery and primitive arrowheads, the Back children were soon making money of their own selling their finds to paying guests. Millie and her sisters even devised a scheme of dunking

 old horseshoes in the spring water until they were encrusted with lime, then convincing naïve sightseers they were "petrified" relics.

With no fish in the old pond, Bill Back introduced bluegill and catfish, but they never survived for long. The carbon dioxide in the water traveled through the gills of the fish and into their bloodstream, killing them almost as soon as they were placed in the water.

Wildlife, on the other hand, thrived around the well. Delighted tourists were spellbound if they spotted a far-off mountain lion or sharp-nosed javelina. Owls, muskrats, porcupines, raccoons, beavers, deer, and several species of snakes also made their homes around the big puddle. Occasionally a flock of egrets stopped by; even blue herons and Canadian geese visited sporadically. The verdant water hole remains a magnificent oasis surrounded by a glorious myriad of flora and fauna.

Millie eventually outgrew the little schoolhouse along Beaver Creek and attended high school in Flagstaff. She went on to Northern Arizona Normal School, a teachers' college that later became Northern Arizona State University.

In 1902, Mildred Back married Granville (Dan) Fain, whose ranching family had been in Arizona since 1874. Norman William Fain was born in 1907, but the marriage did not last and the couple divorced in 1920.

Millie took her son to Prescott to attend school, and later she and Norman moved to Palo Alto, California, where Norman matriculated at Stanford University. While in California, Millie worked at the Stanford Children's Convalescent Home. After Norman graduated from college, mother and son returned to Prescott Valley and together ran the Diamond S Ranch.

Mildred Back Fain died in Prescott on January 13, 1967. Her journey through life was strong and courageous, just like the wild ride she had made so many years ago escaping the horse thieves languishing along the banks of Beaver Creek. In one of the last letters she wrote to her family, she told them she was "off on a new adventure. Don't grieve for you know I always liked a trip and I hope this one will be the best one ever; and I'll just make the trail a little wider for you when you come along."

The venerable spring located on the land of Millie's childhood home continues to run down into Beaver Creek. Montezuma Well became a National Monument in 1906. In 1947 the National Park Service purchased the well and continues to maintain and manage it, along with neighboring Montezuma's Castle.

Wildflowers still bloom along the banks of the limestone-encrusted lake. Owls, hawks, and road-runners nest along its banks, while fox, coyote, and javelina also visit the old water hole. But few mountain lions are left to stop by for a drink.

GRAND CANYON WRANGLER

Edith Jane Bass (Lauzon)
1896–1924

As Mac ambled along the rocky, treacherous trail into
the precipitous depths of the Grand Canyon, he seemed
to understand he was carrying delicate cargo on his back.
The trusty horse tried to keep a smooth, steady stride so
his little passenger would not fall and plunge into the
abyss that lay before horse and rider. Proudly sitting
straight and tall in the saddle, bubbling with excitement
as she journeyed farther and farther along the barely
visible path, three-and-one-half-year-old Edith Jane Bass

saw, for the first time, the imposing surroundings of the majestic Grand
Canyon. Whether she understood what
lay before her, the view deeply rooted
itself in her mind and soul, for the little
girl bouncing along on the big steed,
her soft brown curly ringlets dancing
between sunbeams, never left the canyon
for long. The splendor and beauty of the vista
that stretched beyond the horizon always called her back
and would become the reckoning force that directed the
rest of her life.

Edith's mother, Ada Bass, watched proudly as her
daughter paraded down the winding trail on her first trip
into the canyon. If she had known that her daughter
would spend the rest of her life traveling up and down
the slippery-sloped walls of this vast and infinite gorge—
herding supplies, horses, mules, and
tourists to a myriad of destinations—
Ada might have stopped right in
the middle of the path and taken
her child back to East Worchester,
New York, where she had been born.

The Grand Canyon in northern Arizona, one of the last unexplored areas of the United States, was not yet the romantic, sightseers' delight it would shortly become. In 1869, explorer and Civil War Major John Wesley Powell became one of the first men to travel down the Colorado River below the canyon's majestic, towering embankments. His notes provided necessary data to map the canyon's countless passageways, waterways, flora, and fauna.

In the 1880s, stagecoach, horse, mule, and foot travel were the only means of getting to the canyon; the railroad would not arrive until 1901. Miners prospected in the ravine with dreams of discovering rich lodes of ore, but most left with their dreams unfulfilled. Some of those who stayed soon realized that the sightseeing industry might be more profitable than searching for elusive ores, and turned mining campsites into tourist housing.

One of these men was Edith's father, William W. Bass. A sickly man when he arrived in northern Arizona in 1883, Bass had hoped to improve his health and his wealth by prospecting, but determined that catering to tourists would be more lucrative than any ore he might find in the giant fissure. By the time Edith was born in

1896, he had already established one of the first tourist businesses at the Grand Canyon.

Ada Diefendorf married William Bass in 1895 and became a reluctant hostess in his burgeoning tourist company. When she was due to give birth to their first child, Ada returned to her family home in East Worchester, New York. Proper medical care was not yet an integral part of the vast wilderness in northern Arizona.

Edith Jane was born on August 22, 1896, and it took William three years to convince Ada to return to the canyon with their daughter. Once William convinced Ada to return, he instilled in Edith the excitement he experienced with each breathtaking ride into the Grand Canyon, the thrill of watching the sun rise and set against the stately sheer walls, and the hard work it took eking out a living on this beautiful land. After her first trip down the canyon, Edith was forever captivated with its beauty and grandeur. She considered the length and breadth of the Grand Canyon her playground.

In January 1900, when Edith first rode down the canyon trail, there were few full-time residents along the upper rim. That winter, the weather was so cold in the frost-laden higher regions that mother and daughter headed to Shinumo Camp at the bottom of the vast crevice where temperatures were more temperate and tolerable.

To accommodate tourists he had been transporting into the canyon since 1885, William Bass established Shinumo Camp at the base of the canyon on the far side of the Colorado River. His customers stayed in tents or out in the open beside the outdoor fireplace he built. He also constructed a dining table out of sandstone, fashioning table legs from two large rocks. And he served his customers fresh-caught meat, plus fruits and vegetables grown in the gardens he planted along Shinumo Creek.

As the warmth of spring thawed the upper expanses of the canyon, the family returned to the rim to spend the spring and summer months among the wildflowers and towering pines that edged the perimeter of one most spectacular wonders of the world.

Ada may have wished for a more refined life for her daughter than the wilds of northern Arizona, for in the summer of 1901, she took little Edith and her one-year-old son Billy back East to visit her family. Returning to the canyon later that year, Ada arrived with only Billy in tow. She had left Edith with her mother so the little girl could acquire a proper education. The population at the canyon remained too small to warrant a school until 1911.

While Edith was gone, rail travel arrived at the Grand Canyon bringing adventurers, explorers, vacationers, and the curious to the edge of the abyss. The Santa Fe and Grand Canyon Railway inaugurated its first run from the town of Williams to the Grand Canyon, about a seventy-mile trip, on September 17, 1901. Now the ride that used to take two days by bumpy stage could be traveled in a mere three hours.

William transported incoming passengers from a railroad stop about four miles from the rim, known as Bass Siding, to Bass Camp, his main tourist encampment that lay about twenty-seven miles west of present-day Grand Canyon Village. The railroad encouraged William to advertise his burgeoning business on its trains, even providing passes for the Bass family to travel by rail wherever they cared to go. Ada took advantage of this free transportation and traveled back East whenever possible.

Edith returned to the canyon the following year and by the age of eight, she was spending most of her days

riding down the canyon to round up
horses and mules for the pleasure of
her father's customers entrenched
at Shinumo Camp. She dug vegetables out of the Shinumo Creek garden, picked fruit from the orchard,

loved to paint anything that showed signs
of wear, and watched over her three younger siblings:
Billy, Hazel, and Mabel. Even at this young age, Edith
recognized that her father relied on her to help run the
family business.

Although she often worked long, hard hours tending
to the needs of visitors at her father's tourist camps, plus
following her father's barrage of orders, Edith sometimes
wandered off with her brother and sisters to enjoy the
sun-filled meadows that surrounded their splendid home.

"It was a rather beautiful life," Billy Bass wrote in his
later years. ". . . we gathered wildflowers, we found arrowheads, we built imaginary farms and ranches with barns
and corrals. Wild buckwheat stems would be our mares,
another plant the stallions, small sticks of different colors
our colts. Yucca stems that had moisture in them would
be our cows."

According to her brother, Edith dreamed of the day that she would own her own ranch and herd of horses. Her father gave her several horses during her childhood years, and she even had her own brand, the "E-B." She willingly climbed onto the back of any seasoned or unseasoned mount.

After her first year of schooling back East, Edith studied at a variety of institutions. Ada, who had received her teaching certificate while living in East Worchester, taught her children the basics of reading, writing, and arithmetic, and instilled in them her love of music.

In 1904, Edith was sent to the town of Williams to live with friends and attend school. Some years Ada took the children to Phoenix and lived there during the school year. When at the canyon, however, Edith was often obliged to stay home rather than go to school if help was needed at the house or at one of the campsites. In her diary, Ada often lamented about the demands put on her oldest child, calling Edith "the poor kid." Working in the family business ". . . that is the way she will get an education," Ada wrote.

But Edith always learned best when she was riding sidesaddle on her horse showing newcomers the wonders of the Grand Canyon, the only school she was eager to attend. At the age of ten, she was often sent alone down Canyon trails with fresh horses to meet returning sightseers at the river.

In 1906, William Bass completed work at Bass Siding on a new home for his family that was known as the White House. The White House also became the base of operations for his tourist business, with overnight guests spending enjoyable evenings listening to Ada play the piano and William the violin. The children relished having their own rooms at last, except when their father brought home an overflow of guests. Then, according to Billy Bass, "We'd get up and light the light and fix beds for everybody, and sometimes we kids would have to move out of our beds to make room for the tourists, sleep on the floor if he brought too many people, sleep on the floor or out in the tents."

In August 1906, Mr. and Mrs. Binders arrived at the White House from Atlantic City, New Jersey. The two visitors took notice of ten-year-old Edith's artistic abilities and offered to take the child back to Atlantic City with them where she could attend art school and learn the intricate talent of china painting. Edith went with the Binders but sorely missed her active life at the Canyon. Within a few months, she returned to assume her share of the burden of running the family business. Day after day, Edith rode the Canyon and loved every minute she was in and around the spectacular gorge.

By the time she was thirteen, she could compete with just about any cowboy when it came to wrangling stubborn mules, having acquired the skills of an accomplished roper at an even earlier age. As a wrangler, Edith awoke with the rest of the crew before the sun rose above the Canyon walls. She fed the horses and mules, swept out their stalls, and groomed them for the day's outings.

Once the sightseers saddled up, Edith and the rest of the wranglers headed out with their tenderfoots lined up behind them for the day's excursions. As they traipsed along ancient trails, Edith regaled her charges with her knowledge of the history of the Grand Canyon.

She described the variety of trees, plants, and flowers they encountered, told entertaining stories to her guests, and stayed alert for any crises her companions might encounter, whether it be horse, mule, or rider. Edith Jane

Bass is recognized as the first female wrangler at the Grand Canyon.

By now, she was a necessary part of her father's business. If asked to help with household chores, she chose those that took her outside caring for the goats and chickens and turkeys. She watered the horses, gardened, painted wagons, and of course, jumped on a horse every chance possible. She cheerfully volunteered to travel miles to fetch the mail or bring home supplies. Her favorite task by far was showing off the sights of the beautiful Canyon to tourists and watching the faces of first-time visitors erupt with awe and excitement when they came upon the rim that looked out over the edge of the world.

In 1908, the Grand Canyon was designated a national monument and tourists flocked to the big ravine. Almost every day, Edith pulled on her riding boots, donned a utilitarian denim skirt, plopped a wide-brimmed hat on her head to keep the sun at bay, pulled on her gloves, and set out to hunt, rope, drive wagons, whatever was necessary to keep the tourists happy. She never complained about the workload even when the men left her with disagreeable camp chores as they rode off on a hunting spree. She feared little and learned to cope with unpredictable weather, scarce food supplies, venomous creatures as well as large grizzlies and mountain lions, and sometimes found herself with no place to lay her head at night.

Although she occasionally wandered into unfamiliar territory, she seldom considered herself lost and always managed to find her way back to camp. There came a day, however, when she almost didn't return.

With the campsite secure, sixteen-year-old Edith had a little time before she was needed. She jumped on Fox— a decidedly spirited horse, yet Edith enjoyed his darts and dashes, letting the horse take the lead occasionally. Fox started and scampered, sprinted and bolted, and finally tore into a full gallop, racing across the plain with Edith barely hanging on. The tree came up sharply.

Edith either met the low hanging branch head-on or jumped off the runaway horse, striking her head when she fell. How long she lay unconscious, she had no idea. Gingerly standing on unsteady legs, she took a few tentative steps, decided she suffered no broken bones, and set out back to camp.

What a sight she presented to the horrified tourists! Bruised, bloodied, and scarred, Edith gratefully placed herself into the hands of one of the campers, a doctor who tended to her injuries. Her back was a bothersome nuisance for about a year after the accident, but not enough of a concern to keep her off a horse.

She took somewhat less of a beating the next time she ran into trouble. As the horse took off at her spirited urging, neither girl nor horse saw the wire stretched taut across the fence gate. Approaching at an alarming pace, the horse suddenly stopped short, tossing Edith over his neck. With her face once again suffering the brunt of the fall, she bore the scars from this incident the rest of her life.

To accommodate his growing business, William built another house in 1912 just 100 feet from the rim of the canyon that became known as the Tin House because of the pressed tin covering the exterior walls. The children attended the new school that had been built at the canyon.

At age seventeen, Edith's parents made one last attempt to solidify her education by sending her to school in Oakland, California. They also may have been trying to put some distance between her and a handsome young man William had hired. Bert Lauzon was a proficient guide and horse trainer, and William needed him even more while Edith was away at school. William was not at all happy that his two best hands had formed a more than casual friendship.

The letters written by Edith and Bert Lauzon during the time they were apart were composed with an honest simplicity. In one note, Bert expressed his love as only he knew how: "If I had a stake big enough so we could live happy for ever after I would go up and get you tomorrow and we would get a ranch with some water and plenty of room on the outside for the cows and horses to roam over and have a fine time for ever and ever . . ." "The city life is no good. Look out for autos and cars and don't get run over . . ." "I wish I was there with you so I could get some of those good pickles and something good to eat . . ." "You always look the prettiest girl in the world to me."

Poor Edith was not faring much better: "I am so lonesome right now I can't hardly keep from crying," she wrote. "I am getting awful tired of staying down here without a horse or anything to do that I like to do. I am getting anxious to see you and talk to you. I am awful lonesome for you . . ." "Am sure sick of this city life, don't believe I would ever like it."

William's objection to the union between Edith and Bert Lauzon met with fierce opposition from the young lovers, and on September 21, 1916, the couple married. For the next eight years, Edith and Bert continued to live at the Grand Canyon, most of the time occupying the old White House at Bass Siding that William had built in 1906. They had three children and seemed destined to enjoy a blissful life along the brink of the magnificent landscape the couple mutually adored. By now, the Grand Canyon had become a national park.

Tragically, at the age of twenty-eight, on September 21, 1924, Edith unexpectedly died after surgery. It was her eighth wedding anniversary.

Edith Jane Bass reveled in the wildness of the Grand Canyon. She mastered its intricacies and relished its inconsistencies. The resplendent expanse embraced her and welcomed her. She and the Canyon were one.

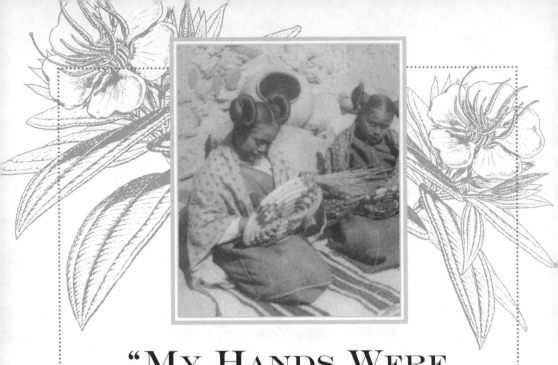

"MY HANDS WERE NEVER STILL"

Helen "Dowawisnima" (Sekaquaptewa)
1898–1990

"Get out! Get out!" the men shouted. "Take your possessions and leave the village! You are no longer part of the
community!"

Fleeing before the shouting men, Dowawisnima
(Dew-wow-iss-nima) clung to her mother's skirts as they
hastened ahead of the men pushing and prodding them
to move faster. She rubbed the bruises and scratches she
had sustained when the men invaded their home, but her
mother kept her moving at a pace almost too fast for the

little girl to keep up. Scared and sore, Dowawisnima stumbled along, not comprehending why they were being forced to the edge of their village. Looking around, she realized many of her friends were also being escorted out of town.

The heightened confusion permeating the Hopi village of Orabi was the result of a rift within the community that had festered for many years. One problem involved the "Hostiles," people of the village who preferred to raise their children at home without assimilation into white society. The "Friendlies," those who supported white ideas, insisted they could no longer live beside Hostiles. The Friendlies overpowered the Hostiles, including Dowawisnima's family, and drove them from their homes.

As she struggled to keep up with her mother, Dowawisnima worried she might never see her home again, or taste the sweet corn her father grew. Orabi was the only home she had known since her birth six years ago.

Twenty days after her birth in 1898, Dowawisnima's mother, Sehynim, and her paternal grandmother carried the newborn to the far eastern edge of the Hopi mesa. As dawn broke over the horizon, the two women asked the sun to bless this little girl and grant her life, health, and a family. The baby was named Dowawisnima, meaning "trail marked by sand." Her life within the Hopi community could now begin, but it would be a life filled with change and controversy.

Hopi communities sit atop three sandstone mesas in northeastern Arizona. Orabi, one of the oldest continuously inhabited villages in the United States, stands on Third Mesa surrounded on three sides by towering, almost unscaleable cliffs.

Dowawisnima's house was built several stories high. As the lower rooms became unstable, thereby unlivable, unused food particles such as melon and squash seeds, peach pits, and leftover corn were dumped into these rooms and preserved in ashes. If a year came when the crops failed and famine threatened, this storeroom provided much needed nourishment until a new bounty of fruits and vegetables could be planted and harvested.

Corn was the staple of the Hopi diet, and young girls learned the techniques of grinding corn from their mothers. Five-year-old Dowawisnima, her raven hair just starting to trail below her shoulders and her deep dark eyes

absorbing everything that lay before her,
received her first lesson in corn grinding
from Sehynim with the results just
good enough to feed the chickens.
Her time to learn the ways of all
Hopi women had begun.

But events interfered with
her instruction, events that
would change Dowawisnima's future forever.

About the time Dowawisnima turned six, a small day
school had been built below the mesa. White authorities
insisted every Hopi child must attend school.
Dowawisnima's parents refused to send their children to
be educated by white teachers. Each day when authorities
climbed the steep incline to take the children to school,
Sehynim hid her children.

Lying on her stomach amid the watermelon seeds and
peach pits in the lower room of the house, Dowawisnima
peered through a hole in the wall and watched as those
looking to tear her away from her family searched for the
children hidden by their parents.

Some days she was spirited away with other girls to
hide in the cornfields. Another time, she would be led

into the hills far from the village. Once she was left behind and had to flee with the boys. But she didn't like the games the boys played and cried until she was allowed to go home and play with her bone dolls.

In return for turning their children over to school authorities, Friendlies received a hoe, an ax, and a shovel or rake, giving them more efficient tools with which to work the land. But even the promise of better tools did not deter the Hostiles from hiding their children.

Eventually, Dowawisnima and the rest of the children were caught and sent to school. She wrote about her first day at the white school in her book, *Me and Mine: The Life Story of Helen Sekaquaptewa*:

First, each was given a bath by one of the Indian women who worked at the school. Baths were given in the kitchen in a round, galvanized tub. Then we were clothed in cotton underwear, cotton dresses, and long black stockings and heavy shoes, furnished by the government. Each week we had a bath and a complete change of clothing. We were permitted to wear the clothes home each day, but my mother took off the clothes of the detested white man as soon as I got home, until it was time to go to school the next day.

Pinned to Dowawisnima's freshly washed cotton dress was a sign that read "Helen," her new American name.

With no books to read, the teacher used objects around the room to teach the children English: desk, chair, window, pencil. Hopi mothers instructed their children not to accept pencils as that meant they consented to white teachings.

At first, Dowawisnima, now called Helen, wanted no part of the white school, but she soon discovered she learned quickly and began looking forward to each day's lessons.

She also grew to prefer the soft cotton clothing distributed by the school rather than the rough woolen, woven garments made by Hopi men.

Hopi males were the community weavers and Dowawisnima remembered her father, Talashongnewa, spending hours before his loom. "When his supplies of corn and beans were getting low," she said, "my father would take a [handwoven] blanket one hundred miles to Winslow, where he would trade it for ten dollars worth of flour, sugar, and salt, which he brought back on his donkey. Father kept his loom humming so that he would be able to keep his family from starving."

Helen spent only one session at school before tempers mounted between the Hostiles and Friendlies, culminating in the ouster of the Hostiles from Orabi in September 1906.

As the Friendlies barged into the house, Dowawisnima remembered one man in particular "because his neck was crooked and he was more fierce and began pushing us, and as he shoved me I fell and rolled down the steps."

The displaced Hostile families settled near Hotevilla Spring, about five miles from Orabi, where the new community of Hotevilla developed and thrived.

The following October, school authorities marched into Hotevilla and rounded up children to be sent to Keams Canyon Boarding School, about forty miles away. Eighty-two children, including Helen, were loaded into wagons for a two-day, very bumpy ride.

Only soft moonlight lit the sky by the time the wagons stopped at Keams Canyon School. Helen, one of the youngest children, stood spellbound as she entered the large dormitory, her new home. She had never before experienced electric light.

I had never seen so much light at night. I was all mixed up and thought it was daytime because it was so light. Pretty soon they gave us hardtack and syrup to eat. There were not enough beds, so they put mattresses on the floor. When I was lying down I looked up and saw where the light came from just before the matron turned out the lights.

"We didn't understand a word of English," Helen remembered, "and didn't know what to say or do." Once again, the clothing her father had woven for her was taken away and replaced with cotton dresses.

Oatmeal mush and bread with little or no milk or sugar greeted Helen her first morning at Keams Canyon School. The much-heartier noon meal usually consisted of beef, potatoes and gravy, with prunes or bread pudding for dessert. Leftovers made up the evening meal.

Food was a bargaining tool, and at first Helen suffered

along with the other little ones when older children, from a variety of tribes, raced to the dining hall and gathered up all the food. She "was always hungry and wanted to cry."

Evenings were the hardest. Helen recalled the little girls "would gather in a corner and cry softly so the matron would not hear and scold or spank us. I would try to be a comforter, but in a little while I would be crying too."

When school let out that first summer, Helen eagerly watched as parents pulled up in wagons to take their children home. But Hostile parents refused to promise they would return their children in the fall, so authorities would not allow Hostile students to leave the school. Helen remained at school throughout the summer with twenty other Hostile girls and six boys.

The next year, Helen's mother came to visit. Since she had to walk most of the way, her visits were few, only two in the four years Helen spent at Keams Canyon. Her godmother came more often and both women brought delicious homemade foods to sustain the child through the school year. They even brought some of her bone dolls from home, toys not easily acquired. Helen recalled how bone dolls were crafted:

Every Hopi girl had an assortment of bones that became her dolls. These bones came from the lower parts of the legs of the sheep. A two-inch was a man doll. A smaller one was the woman. The same bones from smaller animals were the children. Chickens were triangular-shaped bones from the horny hoof. When the sheep was slaughtered, the last four inches of the legs were singed, scraped, and cleaned white, and used to flavor a pot of boiled hominy . . . As a member of the family ate clean such a bone, it would be given to the little girl, as is done with the wishbone from a chicken or turkey. After the bone was dried in the sun, it was white and pretty like ivory.

Saturday was hair-washing day at school. After lining up ("Seems like that was the first English we learned," Helen said, "'Get in line, get in line'"), the matron dipped her fingers in a bowl of kerosene and rubbed the child's hair and scalp before untangling it with a fine-toothed comb that got rid of the "nits." If the comb did not come out clean, the child was sent to the "buggy bench" to receive another treatment of kerosene and more combing until the nits were gone.

Discipline was strict, and Helen remembered many

times she was on the wrong end of a powerful hand. Incorrect answers in the classroom were met with a blow to the head or hand. Helen received so many slaps that after a while she could no longer hear well from one ear.

In the summer of 1910, all the children were allowed to go home. That fall, the Hostiles refused to return their children to school.

Now twelve years old, Helen understood that this extended time at home would probably be her last chance to learn the customs of her people. She already knew how to grind corn; now she would learn the intricacies of cooking piki and curing a piki stone. According to Helen, "It is a lucky girl who inherits a piki stone from her mother."

Piki stones measure about twenty inches wide, two to three inches thick. After hours of smoothing and polishing, the stone is placed over a fire to burn all day before finely ground roasted watermelon or muskmelon seeds are sprinkled over it. Oils released by the seeds turn the stone black and shiny. Piki batter, a paper-thin dough made from cornflower, is spread over the hot stone to cook.

In September 1911, school authorities, accompanied by soldiers, again came to take the children back to

Keams Canyon School. From then on, authorities refused to allow Hostile children to return home during the summer months.

A new school superintendent had taken over Keams Canyon and his ideas of how Hopi children should be treated kept the students on edge. "If I had my way," he told them, "you would never see your homes again. You would live like white people."

Older children had morning lessons and worked at the school in the afternoons. Work assignments were supposed to rotate every three months, but almost always thirteen-year-old Helen was relegated to cleaning bathrooms.

She finally graduated from bathroom cleaning to taking charge of the laundry room where she earned her first salary, fifteen dollars a month. Helen was an industrious worker and saved almost every penny she earned. She even scavenged around the sewing room for leftover scraps of material to make quilt tops, which she sold in town. During the fall, she collected and sold piñon nuts.

Her schoolwork became the pride of Keams Canyon School. "The teachers favored me," she said, "and whenever visitors came they always called on me to recite. I was not the most popular girl in school and my ability did not help me socially, it only made the others jealous." But she was proud of her education and continued to excel in her work.

In 1915, she completed the sixth grade, as far as she could go at Keams Canyon. Hearing about an Indian school in Phoenix, Helen was determined to continue her education. But she needed her parents' permission to go to Phoenix Indian School, and she knew they would never allow her to go so far from home.

She found other students who also wanted to continue their education, and the group confronted the Keams Canyon superintendent, suggesting he fudge a little on their ages, making them old enough to go without parental consent. The superintendent agreed.

Excited and elated, Helen headed home that summer to tell her parents of her plans. But she felt almost a stranger within her family since she had been away at school for so long.

In the fall, she headed for Phoenix Indian School with about seventy other students. Chaperoned by a matron, the children traveled by horse and wagon for two days to Holbrook, then by train to Flagstaff, down through Prescott, finally arriving in Phoenix.

Designed in 1891 as a vocational as well as academic institution, the Phoenix Indian School emphasized manual labor and farming.

Military precision was the key to education and discipline at the school. Uniforms, marching, time-regulated scheduling, neatness, and cleanliness controlled the children's days from sunrise to sunset. A steam whistle signified when to get up, when to eat, when to start school, when to work, and when the day ended. "Everything was done on schedule," Helen remembered, "and there was no time for idleness."

She thrived on the discipline. Not only did she shine in class, but she also caught the eye of School Superintendent John B. Brown who picked Helen to help his wife at home. For five dollars a month, Helen cared for the Brown children and cleaned house. The Browns relied so much on her that they often left her in charge of the entire household while they were away. And although it was the policy for students to change jobs every few months, the Browns managed to keep Helen with them for two years before she was reassigned to the school's sewing department.

Helen "Dowawisnima" (Sekaquaptewa)

Although she never neglected her studies, Helen also made and sold embroidery, crochet, and tatting articles to earn extra money. She prided herself on saving all she could, with thread her most extravagant purchase. She even made shirts for Superintendent Brown and his son. "[M]y hands were never still," she said.

Not all students flourished as did Helen, and punishment was meted out methodically and brutally. The unruly were whipped into conformity. Boys who ran away spent time in the school jail, had their heads shaved, or were forced to wear dresses. Runaway girls were ordered to cut grass with scissors while wearing a card that read, "I ran away" to deter others from attempting to flee back to the reservation.

When Helen completed the eighth grade, she decided it was time to go home. Mrs. Brown begged her to stay, even offering to buy her a sewing machine if she would continue to run the Brown household. But Helen knew she must return to her homeland.

She had met her future husband, Emory Sekaquaptewa, at Phoenix Indian School, and the couple wanted to return to Third Mesa before marrying. But she once again found herself a stranger in her parents' home. Her brother ordered her to take off the soft clothing she had grown to love, presenting her with two fine Hopi costumes he had woven especially for her. She found them "nice and fine and warm and scratchy. I didn't wear them . . ."

On February 14, 1919, Helen married Emory Sekaquaptewa. They had ten children and two foster children, most surviving to adulthood and going on to higher education.

The couple lived in Hotevilla for a while but eventually moved to a ranch near the Hopi-Navajo Reservation border.

"Our lives were a combination of what we thought was the good of both cultures," Helen said. "The Hopi way and what we had learned in school."

Helen "Dowawisnima" Sekaquapetwa died in 1990. She left behind a legacy of hope and hard work for her own children as well as for other Hopi students who wished to continue the Hopi way of life while striving to understand and accept the other world in which they must live.

Dasube (daw-su-be) is a Hopi word that means a rose light that flows in the western sky after sundown and continues on even into the night. Helen remains a guiding force for her people, lighting the way for them to excel while remaining true to their own culture.

LISTEN TO THE SILENCE

Eva Antonia Wilbur (Cruce)
1904–1998

Eva stood her ground. She told the ranch hand to drive
the cattle up the road, but Federico insisted on going by
way of the creek. "I am driving this cattle, not my Father,
not you, either," Eva stormed. "I don't pay you to tell me
what to do. I pay you to do what I tell you do to."
Federico again disagreed with Eva's order, and that was
enough for the fiery cowgirl. She dismissed him on the
spot and took off after the wandering herd.

Stopping to dismount from her horse and close the
gate as the cattle headed down the road, she threw her
right leg over her saddle. Her rowel, the sharp-toothed

wheel at the end of her spur, caught and tangled in the horse's tail. Blue Del, a difficult horse to ride even though Eva like his spirited nature, reared up at the sudden pain in his buttocks and took off at a terrifying pace.

Standing with her left foot still in the stirrup, one hand on the saddle horn and the other holding tight to the reins, Eva struggled to release her right foot from the horse's tail as Blue Del bolted. She knew with dreadful certainty that "a rider with a foot tied to a horse's tail was as good as dead."

The clamor of hysterical horse and panicky rider reached the ears of Federico as he sauntered along the trail. Realizing the danger his ex-boss was in, the cowboy dashed toward the horse and grabbed the reins. But the distressed steed wanted rid of whatever was causing his pain and continued to buck and rear to be free of his tormentor. "The more he fought," said Eva, "the more I pulled his tail . . . ."

Finally, Federico managed to get a handkerchief over Blue Del's eyes and calmed the frightened horse enough for Eva to slip out of her boot and onto the ground. Shaking and trembling, she plopped down, waiting for her heart to stop its terrifying pounding.

The rowel was embedded deeply in the horse's tail, and Federico cut off a good portion of Blue Del's hair before returning the boot to Eva. He could tell she was about to faint, lose her breakfast, or both, and assured her he would stay until she composed herself. Accepting her thanks, the cowboy knew he had just been rehired.

"You hire them and you fire them," her father had instructed Eva when he put her in charge during his absence. "But I will hold you responsible for anything that goes wrong. No giggling and no crying!" Eva Antonia Wilbur was barely ten years old.

Through the years, Eva learned to "lift myself up by my bootstraps, and lick my wounds in silence. I did not dare tell Father about my painful experiences, as it would only anger and antagonize him." Her father's approval meant the world to Eva from the first time he lifted his young daughter onto a horse.

Born on February 22, 1904 to Augustín and Ramona Wilbur, Eva adored her father, "and I wanted nothing more than to be just like him." Years later, she wrote the memories of her childhood on the Wilbur ranch in her book, *A Beautiful, Cruel County*. She described her young life as "fenced in. I had no social life whatsoever. The only friends I had were the Indians until they too left. My father did not allow us to go to school in Arivaca. It's very difficult to grow up like that . . . "

The Wilbur Ranch, homesteaded in the mid-1800s by Eva's grandfather, Dr. Ruben Augustine Wilbur, lay in southern Arizona near the town of Arivaca. It was surrounded by resplendent mountains, a water supply gleaned from sporadic watering holes and a nearby creek, a magnificent cottonwood forest, and hundreds of Indians, mainly Tohono O'Odham. Lions, antelope, deer, thousands of burros, a multitude of small creatures, and a rainbow of birds roamed across and nested on the Wilbur ranchland.

Along with raising cattle and goats, Dr. Wilbur purchased twenty-five mares and a stallion from a horse trader traveling up from Mexico, horses called Spanish barbs that were probably direct descendants of those brought from Spain in the late 1600s. Cowboys called the sturdy steeds rock horses because they could climb steep rock-strewn slopes with ease, and had hooves so hard they could not be shod.

Eva's father, Augustín Wilbur, lived and worked on the ranch his entire life, and expected his oldest daughter to follow his boots and absorb all he taught her.

Her playmates were the Indian children living nearby. Wahyanita, several years older than Eva, taught her the ways of the Indians—such as how to locate the best prayer sticks, instruments Wahyanita proclaimed were more powerful than Augustín's deadly rifle.

Seven-year-old Dreyah liked to sneak up behind Eva and pinch her rear. When Eva complained to her father, Augustín berated her for not fighting back and told her she would feel the sting of his *reata*, or lasso, if she did not stick up for herself.

The next time Dreyah pinched her, Eva picked up a large bone and smacked the girl in the head. As the child sank to the ground, Eva ran screaming she had killed her friend. By the time her mother reached the fallen child, Dreyah was sitting up nursing her wound. She never pinched Eva again.

"We still had fights and threw rocks at each other, but at noon we stormed the kitchen together for whatever lunch Mother could dispense."

Eva faced a dilemma when she was charged with the care of her younger sister Ruby. " . . . [N]o matter what blows I received at Ruby's hands, I could endure them because I was a big girl."

But when Wahyanita became angry and whipped her with a willow branch, her mother told her she was too little to play with the older child.

"So I had to endure the blows from Ruby because I was a big girl and the whippings from Wahyanita because I was too little, just a baby."

Five-year-old Eva begged her father to take her to the top of El Cerro, a rocky, rugged hill that would eventually become her refuge from the rages and tirades of the demanding Augustín. She argued she was a big girl now and could handle the rough terrain and not cry if she got tired. While her mother argued she was too small for such a trip, Augustín put Eva up behind him on Diamante, one of the rock horses, and the two set out toward the towering rise.

Along the trail, they came upon a calf suffering from a festering wound filled with squiggly maggots. Augustín poured pungent creosote liquid into the wound and the worms magically disappeared. Digging into the lesion to dislodge the remaining grubs, the calf bawled and struggled to be free. Augustín instructed Eva to remove the remaining maggots.

Fearfully, she moved toward the calf. "I put my finger inside the wound and felt the maggots moving against the tip of my finger. I felt sick, retched, and vomited over my father's hand. Vomit ran down the white coat of the calf."

"Toughen up, toughen up," Augustín ordered. "You'll get over it."

Finally the maggots spilled over the ground and Eva's father praised her efforts. "I guess I had toughened up," she remembered. "Good thing I did, for this was one task I had to do many, many times, month after month and year after year."

When she was old enough to handle a horse by herself, her father gave her Diamante.

I took to the trails at will, Diamante my faithful companion, my playmate. But he was also my protector. He would gallop joyfully down the creek with me on his back, but if there were any sign of trouble he would stop, point his ears, turn around, and head for home. Even if I pulled on the reins Diamante would take the bit

*in his teeth and never stop until he had arrived at the
kitchen door.*

As she and Diamante climbed over rocky terrain and
explored around the creek bed, Eva watched and listened,
becoming an expert in the comings and goings of all the
creatures that occupied Wilbur land.

One day Mr. and Mrs. Olson, a surveyor and his wife,
visited the ranch. When the man propounded that a
nearby darkened hill was made from black volcanic rock,
Eva informed the surveyor that the hill was not the product of an underground eruption but actually covered with
black birds—ravens and cowbirds. Dismissing the child's
ramblings, the visitor continued his dissertation on lava
rock. "Just then," said Eva, "as if by magic, the shining
black coverlet lifted from the side of the mountain,
breaking up and flying away in all directions. I felt vindi-
cated and Mr. and Mrs. Olson stood still, transfixed."

According to Eva, when she was four she learned to
drive the stock out to pasture and back into the pens at
night. She first herded goats, then took on the cows.
"There seemed always to be new and more difficult lessons to learn, and I was expected never to show any fear

or signs of weakness." Her father would not tolerate carelessness and often insisted his daughter learn lessons far beyond her abilities.

She spent more and more time along the banks of the creek or riding to the top of El Cerro. However, she could never escape her father's demands, his orders, his tirades.

On one occasion, Augustín told her to head a herd of steers into the corral and not let them get through the gap and wander off. The lead steer, however, had other ideas and headed toward the gap with the other cattle dutifully following. Sitting astride Diamante, the little girl rode into the gap and tried to turn the cattle back toward the corral. When her father appeared over the rise, however, there was not a cow to be seen. The angry sting of his *reata* across her arms and back was his way of teaching her that he would not tolerate sloppy work regardless of her age.

"I followed Father up the wash, my back and arms still burning from the lashing. I put my arms around Diamante's leg and cried heartbrokenly. What had happened to the beautiful man who had taken me to the peak of El Cerro? When Father picked me up and put me in the saddle he held me for a moment, tightly. When he released me tears dropped from his eyes."

Augustín had registered the Wilbur brand, an "E" above a "W," shortly after Eva's birth. She learned to brand cattle at the age of five and had a terrible time discerning between an "E" and the number "3." Her father proclaimed only a *zonza*, a stupid girl, would not know the difference between a letter and a number.

She learned to place a pile of wood so it would produce a strong blaze, and stoked the branding fire to a torrid temperature. As she heated the red-hot branding irons, her father roped a calf and threw it on its side. Racing with the hot poker, Eva held the iron to the calf's side, singeing its short hairs. As Augustín flipped the calf over, she applied the "EW" brand to its other flank.

Eva cared for sick cows, and those pesky maggots were a constant chore. She became an expert in maggot removal. ". . . [W]hen the wound finally appeared clean, I poked it full of horse manure to suffocate whatever worms may have been left."

She wore Levis just like her father. "The mini-Levis were a product of my mother's clever hands, for in those days Levi Strauss did not manufacture pants for women, much less for children. When people saw me dressed in the small Levis they made remarks . . . some kind and some unkind."

She spent long days by herself out on the land checking water holes, looking for lost calves, sometimes riding fifteen miles to the southern end of the Wilbur property near the Mexican border. She found comfort in the birds and animals that met her as she and Diamante made their rounds. "I got in the habit of working alone, and when I got used to the animals and they got used to me, I wasn't alone anymore. They became good friends!"

She watched creatures satiate their thirst at the bubbling creek. When life became too difficult, especially after her father shouted and berated her for something that did not meet his expectations, she escaped to the top of nearby El Cerro, where she probed the artistry of the sky and eavesdropped on the wind.

"I learned to listen to the silence. When you are not alone, you sit and hear, but you don't pay attention to what you hear. When we are alone, ah, that's when we listen, and that's when we hear. We hear the wind sing and nature pulsate."

One day a flock of doves landed near one of the water holes she was repairing. As the birds flew skyward, one dove remained. From then on, whenever she returned to that particular hole, the lone dove sat on a rock in the middle of the water and watched her work.

Eva spied prairie dogs scampering across the rocks, then disappearing, only to pop up a few feet away. Small finches scolded but tolerated her presence. "The quail, the wolf, the coyote—I knew them, and they knew me."

A roadrunner learned to accept food Eva laid down for her. After her babies were born, the roadrunner taught her little chicks to take the scraps Eva offered.

One day she did a strange and touching thing. She flew from the tree to the ground and attacked some tiny creature in the dust, shaking her big round head as she killed her prey. She flitted back into the tree and jumped across my legs, depositing a mutilated praying mantis in my lap. I threw it to the ground, and again she went after it, bringing it back to me. When I finally understood and pretended to eat the unsavory fare she rewarded me with her fluttering cuckoo call.

At a dry water hole, she met a hawk. After she dug in the sand to bring moisture up for the thirsty bird, "[h]e would come whenever I was there."

The second year, he was very friendly; he wasn't afraid of me. He would go right to the water hole; in the center there was a big rock where the hawk would sit and watch me work. I liked that. But when the hawk came, the little prairie dogs got scared and ran away into their dens, even when it was so hot. I felt sorry for them, so I used to throw water at the hawk, but I could never get rid of him. The only way that I could get rid of him was to sing. If I sang, then the hawk would fly up to the hackberry tree and north up to the trail and come back and fly over me, winging fast towards Mexico, where people knew how to sing.

Eva's education centered on learning ranch chores until Augustín's sister Mary took over as teacher for both Eva and sister Ruby. School began precisely at six in the morning and lasted until six at night. The girls sat on a plank in the barn and shared a *pizarra*, or slate.

Eva loved to write, especially poems, but her mother

explained, "A poet is a very highly educated man. You have never seen the inside of a school. People will think you are crazy." From then on, Eva called her poems songs.

When she was thirteen, she went off to the Guardian Angel Convent School in Los Angeles, California. That first year was horrible! She did not know how to interact with other girls, and spent much of her time sitting under the piano in the music room crying her eyes out. The Sisters told the other girls that Eva was "from someplace in Arizona—some wild place . . . You must be kind to her because she doesn't know anything."

By the next year, she learned to make friends and began enjoying her years away from the ranch, away from her father's constant orders and demands. However, she always missed the birds and the animals that ran to greet her when she and Diamante climbed El Cerro or splashed through the creek.

In April 1933, Augustín died after a fall from his horse, and Eva returned to the Wilbur ranch. That same year she married Marshall Cruce and went to live in Tucson.

She spent her weekends at the old ranch in Arivaca trying to maintain the ancient homestead, tending to the goats and cattle, and the sprightly Spanish barb horses.

At the time of his death, Augustín was in the midst of dispute over cattle, land, and water rights, and Eva was soon thrust into the fray pitting neighbor against neighbor. Cattle and horses were killed in retaliation on all sides of the ongoing hostility. Trusting no one, Eva armed herself and was eventually arrested and convicted of killing a horse belonging to someone else, and branding its colt with the "EW" symbol. Sentenced to serve two years in Florence Prison, she entered the penitentiary in May 1944, serving until February 1945 when she was paroled.

Eva and Marshall spent their remaining years protecting the Spanish rock horses that roamed the Wilbur land, but many of them starved to death when the land became severely overgrazed. No one trespassed on Wilbur property without a warning shot from "La Pistolera," the nickname Eva acquired because of her proclivity for shooting at anyone found on her property.

At age eighty-three, she started writing letters to nieces and nephews about life on the ranch. These letters turned into short stories that eventually framed her book, A Beautiful, Cruel Country.

In 1989, the same year her husband died, Eva sold the Wilbur Ranch to the Arizona Nature Conservancy. She retained the house and ten acres, but at age eighty-five, she could no longer maintain even that small acreage. When the government wanted the historic Spanish barb rock horses removed from the land, she turned them over to the American Minor Breeders Conservancy.

Eva Antonia Wilbur Cruce died on February 4, 1998. She knew only the birds and animals as her true friends. She trusted them implicitly as she did no human, and she relied on the solace and comfort they bestowed upon a very lonely girl.

"PLAY BALL!"

The Girls of Summer
1933–Present

Fans excitedly jammed New York City's Madison Square Garden as seventeen-year-old Dottie Wilkinson crouched behind home plate and waited for the first pitch. She wore no protective mask or shin guards, and only recently had started wearing a chest protector. In red satin shorts, Dottie and the rest of her softball team, known as the PBSW Ramblers, received a goodly dose of hoots and hollers from the crowd. Those shouts, however, turned into stunned silence as the Ramblers beat the local favorites, the New York Roverettes, in a hotly contested, eighteen-inning softball game before a crowd of thousands.

The Ramblers, leaving their farming and ranching chores behind in Arizona, descended upon the Big Apple in 1938 and raised the roof of the Garden. They demonstrated the art of girls' softball to a sophisticated New York crowd and won the hearts and accolades of hardened baseball fans.

The PBSW Ramblers, sponsored by the Peterson-Brooke-Steiner-Wist School Supply Company of Phoenix, were first organized in 1933 when Dottie walked onto the field as an eleven-year-old bat girl. Within a short time, she was playing second base against girls more than twice her age. When she moved to catcher position, no one could compete with the little farm girl from south Phoenix. Softball became an obsession and a passion for Dottie as it did for dozens of young girls across Arizona.

Softball, at one time called "indoor baseball played outdoors," has been around since 1887, with women taking up the sport shortly after its inception. Once Amelia Bloomer created her famous pantaloons allow-

ing women to participate in more active endeavors while remaining modestly dressed, the number of girls appearing on playing fields multiplied.

In 1923, Lou Hoover, wife of soon-to-be U.S. President Herbert Hoover, pushed for the formation of the Women's Division of the National Amateur Athletic Federation, which brought forth women's regulations and policies in sports. By 1926, women's rules for playing ball were established since "standard baseball is too strenuous for the weaker sex." Smaller bats were shaped to fit a woman's hands, larger balls constructed, and the restructuring of shorter base paths and pitching distances provided the impetus for softball as it is known today.

However, if a girl injured herself on the field or showed signs of fatigue, she was told to quit the game. No thought was given to conditioning girls to participate in sports.

As the Great Depression of 1929 loomed over the country, followed shortly by the onset of World War II, money became scarce for everyone and paid amusements were forsaken in order to put food on the table. But softball was free and fun, and thousands either played the game or enjoyed watching others toss the ball around, smack it into center field, and dive for the impossible catch. Softball became one of the country's favorite sports.

The first softball championship game took place in Chicago in 1933, the year Dottie Wilkinson started playing for the Ramblers. Almost every team used a different set of rules, and it wasn't until the following year that universal regulations were established for the game.

Dottie became known as the greatest catcher in women's softball. Born on her parents' farm in south Phoenix in 1921, her childhood consisted of household chores and riding her horse Babe. She spent her summers playing ball and was never happier than on the field with her nose just inches from the dust and grime around home plate. She entertained no thoughts of attaining national attention.

As a catcher, Dottie wore little protective gear. "Those days you didn't have a mask," she said. "You just take the glove and go back there and catch. I never did get hurt. I caught the ball." She was eventually issued a chest protector but tore out the stuffing until she had little more than a thin piece of cloth between her and the incoming ball. And although she at first used a catcher's mitt, she ultimately opted for a thinner five-fingered glove to give her hand more flexibility.

Coaches warned their players, "Don't slide into Wilkinson. Just knock her down; she's not going to let you have the plate." Few stole home with Dottie hugging the bag.

Weekend trips out of town put her in the care of older girls on the team and her coach Ford Hoffman, who had organized the Ramblers in 1933. Her older sister Ruth, at age fourteen, also played for the Ramblers a few years but left to marry when Dottie was still a teenager. But her parents trusted Coach Hoffman with the care of their daughter, as did many Arizona families who allowed their girls to travel the state under the coach's guidance and supervision.

When she was thirteen, Dottie and the team headed for Chicago and the National Softball Tournament at Soldier Field. This was her longest trip away from home, about two weeks, and Dottie loved every minute of it.

By 1938 when the team shook the rafters of Madison Square Garden, Dottie was a seasoned veteran taking on the responsibility of watching over younger girls who admired her stamina and athleticism.

One Rambler kept a log of her trip to New York. Excerpts from the log reveal the grueling schedule, but also capture the excitement the girls experienced as they rode across country on the adventure of their lives.

Sept. 1, 1938: We left Phoenix this morning at 5:00 A.M. It's raining cats and dogs. We expect to work out in Gallup, N.M. tonight but if it is raining like it is here, we won't be able to. It is now 12:15 P.M. and our next stop is Winslow.

Sept. 4: We won our game last night [in Tulsa, Oklahoma] 6–4. We passed through a small part of Kansas and we are now at Cuba, Missouri. We now have only about 380 miles to go to Chicago.

Sept. 6: We arrived here in Chicago at 11:30 this morning.

Sept. 7: It is raining hard this morning so I don't know whether we'll work out or not. We went to the show to see "My Lucky Star" with Sonja Henie last night and it cost us 90 cents. It was a good show but not worth 90 cents.

Sept. 8: We went to the big parade last night that they had celebrating the opening of the World Tournament.

Sept. 9: Our game was postponed last night on account of rain. We are still working out every day though—rain or no rain.

Sept.10: We played Oklahoma tonight. We beat 8–6.

Sept. 11: Didn't do much. Played Nebraska at 7:00— won 8–0. Had to wait 4½ hrs. to play Calif. They got breaks and beat 3–2.

Sept. 12: Drove all day; saw beautiful country. We were all dead tired. We had had 3 hrs. sleep in 3 days.

Sept. 13: Drove all day, arrived in N.Y. 7:00 P.M. Played ball at Madison Square Garden and beat 4–1. Sure thrilled—had 10,000 spectators. Will play the team [N.Y. Roverettes] again Thurs., night.

Sept. 14: Had a swell time today. Jack Dempsey had us at his place for lunch. All the girls were so stuffed with souvenirs from his place that they could hardly walk. We were then taken to Radio City where we went through it. Went to Coney Island at night and sure did have fun.

Sept. 15: Played N.Y. Roverettes at Garden—played 18 innings. Finally won 2–0.

Sept. 16: Left N.Y. at 8:00 A.M. Sure tired out.

In 1940, the PBSW Ramblers won the national softball championship, the first Arizona team to bring home a national title in any sport. They repeated their victories in 1948 and 1949.

Dottie Wilkinson was certainly not alone on the ball field. Dozens of young girls made their mark with Arizona's first female softball team.

Amy Peralta pitched over 800 games, winning over 670. She always claimed she "was a good pitcher because I had a good team behind me."

At age eleven, Marjorie Law began her two-decade career playing outfield, first base, third base, and eventually settled in as pitcher earning eight championships. As one player remarked, "When Margie Law hit you with that ball, you wore the writing on that ball for a week!"

Jessie Glasscock joined the team at age fifteen playing shortstop.

One girl conquered more than the ball field when she

joined the Ramblers. At age thirteen, Billie Harris was playing softball with the Sunshine Girls, a recreational team in Tucson, Arizona. Her high school coach had chased her off the school team because "she threw the ball too hard." "It was maddening for someone who wanted to play and be part of a team," Billie lamented.

When the Sunshine Girls traveled to Phoenix in 1950, Billie's pitching prowess and running abilities caught the eye of the Ramblers' coach, and he invited her to join the team. Billie Harris became the first African American to play for the Ramblers.

Raised by a mother who warned her about the prejudice she would face no matter what endeavors she pursued, Billie learned to ignore the adverse notoriety she encountered.

Aware there might be some fan disapproval in recruiting a young black girl to play on an all-white team, Coach Hoffman gradually added Billie to the games; she played an inning here, another there. But the fans loved her fastpitch style and took to her like a ball stuck in a glove.

It was on the road that Billie experienced the stigma of prejudice, bigotry, and intolerance.

Traveling teams usually piled into a couple of cars to head out to the next county or across country. Pulling into a restaurant along the road, Billie never knew if she would be allowed to eat with the team. If she was refused service, the coach continued to order for everyone else. When the food arrived, the entire team walked out of the restaurant leaving the server staring at the swinging door while juggling hot plates of uneaten food. Sometimes, if fans became disruptive when Billie stepped to the mound, every Rambler girl headed into the stands to chastise and chase off the offending hecklers. Fearing problems en route to the 1956 Amateur Softball Association of America World Championship games in Clearwater, Florida, the coach deemed that Billie should stay behind.

"I only wanted to play ball," Billie said. Today, she is deeply concerned that "some people don't believe the things that happened in the past." However, she is quick to add she "had more good experiences than bad."

The Ramblers ruled girls' softball, particularly in Arizona, until 1937 when the A1 Queens team was organized under the tutelage of Coach Larry Walker. The Queens, sponsored by the Arizona Brewing Company, quickly earned the title "the most beautiful softball team in the world." Donning short white satin skirts over even shorter shorts, they played ball just as hard and with just as much passion as their neighboring rivals, the Ramblers.

According to a 1949 *Arizona Highways* magazine article, ". . . girls' softball . . . wasn't just a display of pretty legs and trim figures but found the teams battling one another with unmistakeable [sic] fierceness [which] brought out the fans in droves." On a night when any number of men's teams might be playing in Phoenix, over three thousand fans turned out to watch the Ramblers and Queens compete in a battle of power and will. The competition between the two teams established Phoenix as the "Softball Capital of the World."

In 1947, the Queens conquered the National Softball Congress tournament and walked off the field boasting the largest attendance of the games. Ensuing years found them repeat champions in 1949, 1951, 1952, and 1954.

Both teams often played benefit games in Arizona and on the road. When the Queens played the New Orleans Jax in 1948 to raise money for crippled children, 7,500 spectators showed up. They also traveled out of the country to Hermosillo and Guaymas, Mexico, for exhibition games. No place was too far for the roaming Queens, but Arizona was where they wanted to win, and the Ramblers were who they aimed to beat.

Until 1945 the Ramblers never lost a state championship, but by that time, the Queens were a force of strong, determined girls who were hungry to show they were of equal power and ability to beat the Ramblers. The games between the two rivals often ended in a one-run win or a tie.

Occasionally, a player crossed over from one team to the other. Fourteen-year-old Flora Bell Davies spent her first year playing second base for the Ramblers, then played the remainder of her softball days with the Queens as an outfielder.

In 1939, the Queens followed the Ramblers into Madison Square Garden and Flora Bell went along for the cross-country ride. The girls took off in a couple of cars and played twenty games on the road before arriving in New York. As large as the crowds had been the year before when the Ramblers hit New York City, this year as many as eighteen thousand to twenty thousand fans jammed the Garden to watch the gorgeous Queens take the field. Flora Bell played until 1947, ending her career the year the Queens won the National Softball Congress Championship.

The Queens traveled out of state more than did the Ramblers, and Flora Bell was considered one of the more seasoned players. She watched over younger team members such as Betty Giertz who was fourteen when she began playing for the team in 1941. However, Betty's age did not stop the third-base power hitter from driving the car on some of their cross-country trips.

The Queens often spent one summer month each year traveling east playing mainly men's teams. Each night they would conquer the field, then hit the road for the next town. Arriving around noon, they would play that night, then it was off to their next game. It was a grueling schedule, but young Betty thrived on the excitement. During her tenure with the Queens, she had one twenty-game hitting streak and played in two World championships and three Arizona state championships.

Fourteen-year-old Charlotte "Skippy" Armstrong started playing for the Queens in 1939. She powered her dangerous pitch to six National Softball Congress All-American titles, and three times received honors as Most Outstanding Pitcher. She is also credited with designing one of the glamorous uniforms worn by the girls.

Each night, the team washed their uniforms and briskly polished their scuffed-up shoes. If anyone failed to pass the coach's inspection, he levied a fine upon the slovenly one. He allowed none of his beauty Queens to appear on the ball field wearing a bandage.

One of the A1 Queens played only one season with the team, but her impact on the sport in Arizona remains as strong today as it was over seventy years ago.

Seventeen-year-old Rose Perica defended first base when the Queens conquered Madison Square Garden in 1939. Born in 1922 in Six Shooter Canyon in Globe, Arizona, the youngest of six children, Rose grew up playing softball, tennis, basketball, and running track on the dirt playgrounds in her rural hometown.

Her parents, immigrants from Austria, instilled in their children a zest for life and an indomitable work ethic. Rose often said her mother "could make a dinner out of nothing but a sack of potatoes and some beans."

Never missing a day of school, Rose garnered straight As throughout her school years, was elected the first female class president of Globe High School, and gave the valedictory address for her graduating class after attaining the highest grade point average ever achieved at the school.

She excelled in basketball to the extent she was offered a contract to play for the professional All-American Redheads basketball team. But Rose turned it down, preferring the competition and companionship she experienced on the softball field. "It was a terrific experience," she remembers. "I learned a lot about winning and losing."

While playing for the Queens, Rose was also assisting an up-and-coming politician, Joe Hunt, by distributing petitions for his election as Arizona State Treasurer. Joe promised her a job if he won the election and with her prize-winning typing skills, she soon found herself with a $125-a-month job in the State Treasurer's office.

From her position as secretary in 1940, Rose traveled the ladder of political success to the highest pinnacle. Marrying T. R. "Lefty" Mofford in 1957, she was appointed Arizona Secretary of State in 1977 and won the seat three consecutive terms. In 1988, she took over the governorship of the state when then-governor Evan Mecham was impeached. Rose Perica Mofford became the first woman governor of Arizona.

Throughout her distinguished career, Rose always remembered her days on the ball field. She was instrumental in helping organize the Arizona Softball Foundation and was honored as the Foundation's Woman of the Year in 1976. In 1974, the Arizona Softball Association founded the Hall of Fame. Rose was inducted into the Hall on two separate occasions, once for her playing prowess and later for her support of youth and sports.

During the 1980s, she helped establish the Arizona Baseball Commission and was instrumental in passing legislation bringing the spring-training Cactus League into the state. To this day, Rose remains an integral part of Arizona sports.

Many of the girls who played on the Ramblers and Queens distinguished themselves in a variety of professions and remain active, vital members of their communities. Almost all of them have been honored by induction into the Arizona Softball Hall of Fame. The town of Prescott, Arizona, proudly took over the title of "Softball Capital of the World" when the Hall of Fame was moved there in 2006.

Dottie Wilkinson played softball for thirty-three years. She also won accolades for her bowling expertise and was honored by the Women's International Bowling Congress Hall of Fame. She continues to live in Phoenix where she worked for many years in real estate with her old Ramblers coach, Ford Hoffman.

Billie Harris continues to work for Mesa Community College. Her softball career spanned over twenty-five years. She is the first African-American woman inducted into the National Softball Hall of Fame.

Amy Peralta became a beautician, while Marjorie Law taught school for many years. Charlotte Armstrong is an artist in Scottsdale. Betty Giertz put her energies into making a home for her family, as did Flora Bell Davies who married Queens coach Larry Walker.

Title IX, the legislation passed in 1972 that gave women equal status on ballfields, basketball and tennis courts, and in all other educational activities, states: "No person in the United States shall, on the basis of sex, be excluded from participation in, be denied the benefits of, or be subjected to discrimination under any education program or activity receiving Federal financial assistance . . . "

Mary Littlewood, who served as women's softball coach at Arizona State University in Tempe for nineteen years, understood how much those first girls of summer achieved without the benefit of Title IX legislation. "The significance of Title IX in American society is that culturally, women athletes and girls are accepted, empowered, esteemed and idolized now as compared to their being ridiculed and criticized . . . "

The Arizona girls who comprised those first softball teams during the 1930s, '40s, and '50s played for the love of the sport, and no one could drive them off the ball field. As one article surmised, the girls of summer, particularly the rivalry between the PBSW Ramblers and the A1 Queens, "is hot, and it increases in temperature right along with the summer weather."

While there was no love lost between the two teams during the years they competed, today the PBSW Ramblers and A1 Queens meet annually to joke and jibe at each other about the fierce rivalry they enjoyed. Sometimes an aura of wistfulness envelops them, and one can almost see a yearning in their eyes to revisit the days when their young legs carried them around the bases at top speed, and allowed them to scoop up a ball and throw out a runner tearing toward home plate. The roars and cheers can still be heard echoing across the desert from those long-ago summer days.

No Place to Call Home

Ruth Okimoto (Lipofsky)
1936–Present

In 1942, six-year-old Ruth Okimoto stood in line as she did every day. Sometimes she stood in line for meals, other times just to wash up or use the bathroom. This time, however, the line formed outside the first school-house the little girl would attend. As the doors opened, she waited impatiently to see the neat rows of desks and chairs; the crisp, clean paper and well-sharpened pencils that would challenge her curious mind. And the books! Oh, how she craved to open the books that would show her the world.

Ruth Okimoto (Lipofsky)

Ruth walked into the room and stood in silence as did the rest of the Japanese American children. They surveyed the bare space that lay before them. There were no desks, no chairs, no paper and pencils, and absolutely not one book within the vast, empty room. The internment camp at Poston, Arizona, was not yet ready to educate the children imprisoned behind its barricades in the desolate Southwestern desert. For the little girl on her first day of school, there was nothing for Ruth to do.

On December 7, 1941, Japan attacked the United States at Pearl Harbor, Hawaii, killing over two thousand people and sending tremors of turmoil and apprehension across the continental United States. To establish a semblance of order as the fear of more violence escalated, President Franklin Delano Roosevelt ordered that all people of Japanese descent who were living along the western coasts of Washington, Oregon, and California be relocated to hastily made internment camps. They were stripped of their lands, their homes, their communities, and their liberties.

"None of these people were charged with any crime," said Ruth years later, "other than being of Japanese descent."

The Okimoto family had made their home in San Diego since emigrating from Japan. in 1937, arriving just three days before Ruth's first birthday. Her father, Tameichi Okimoto, was a Christian missionary and had brought his family to the United States where he continued his ministry. Kirie Okimoto, Ruth's mother, was also a missionary as well as a schoolteacher. Although the couple's marriage was an arranged one, with Kirie given a choice between two men, they were happy with their family of two boys and a little girl.

At the beginning of 1942, Ruth was already excited to start school that fall. But by February, President Roosevelt had issued Executive Order No. 9066 authorizing the Secretary of War to exclude individuals from strategic areas and provide them with "transportation, food, shelter, and other accommodations as may be necessary . . ." These orders specifically targeted the Japanese population, and a mass forced evacuation of thousands of Japanese immigrants and Japanese Americans began.

Incarceration of Japanese people in assembly centers started in March 1942. The Okimotos were delayed in leaving their home, however, when Ruth and her brothers came down with the measles. Instead of going by train as did most of the evacuees, the family finally departed on May 1 by means of an old army truck. Told she could take only what she could carry, Ruth clutched her doll as she boarded the rickety vehicle for the 150-mile journey to the Santa Anita Racetrack holding center. Her mother awkwardly climbed in next to her; she was three months from giving birth to her fourth child.

Along with her parents and older brother, Ruth was known as an Issei because they were all born in Japan. Japanese children born in the United States, like her younger brother, were Niseis. Niseis were American citizens, but not until 1952 were native-born Japanese allowed to become American citizens. In 1954, at the age of eighteen, Ruth passed an examination to become a citizen in the country she had lived almost all her life.

Conditions at the Santa Anita Racetrack were far from perfect when Ruth and her family arrived. Since this was a temporary holding center until authorities shipped their charges to hastily built internment camps across the country, little effort was made to improve conditions for the hundreds of people brought to the site. As each group arrived, they were greeted by armed guards who handed them a sleeping cot and showed them where to fill their mattresses with straw. Some families were housed in empty horse stalls that had only been washed down from the previous occupants, allowing a pungent odor to linger in the warm, humid spring air. Ruth's family was assigned to one of the quickly erected barracks. Under these less than sterile conditions, Ruth's mother gave birth to her fourth child, a son.

For more than three long months, hundreds of Japanese languished at Santa Anita. The temperature soared, as did tempers. Interviewed in 2002 by "Face to Face," an interactive educational Web site, Ruth remembered,

> When we went to Santa Anita, we were put in this small little room that had just enough room for five cots and a little aisle way so you could get to the end of the line. And I was on the last cot, next to the wall and there was a window there, a curtainless window. So every night the searchlights would come over the room and periodically the light would just shine into the room. And that I remember vividly 'cause it was hard to sleep.

Finally, on August 28, the detainees were put on a train that took them to Parker, Arizona, just across the border from California along the swift-flowing Colorado River. As they left the train, they boarded buses and trucks for the seventeen-mile journey to Poston Internment Camp, one of ten concentration camps erected across the country to house Japanese Americans. Over one hundred twenty thousand Isseis and Niseis were confined in these prisons, at least two-thirds of them U.S. citizens by birth.

Named after Charles Debrille Poston, Arizona's first superintendent of Indian Affairs, Poston Camp sat on the Colorado River Indian Reservation (CRIR), established in 1865, and home to the Mohave and Chemehuevi Indians, smack in the middle of the desert in one of the hottest spots in the United States. There was little need for armed guards at the camp since it was so isolated. During World Was II, Poston was the third largest city in Arizona, housing around twenty thousand detainees.

As people descended from the trucks and buses to examine their new home, they were greeted with a blast of heat so intense they wondered if they had descended into the depths of Hades. Temperatures in the Arizona desert soared well over one hundred degrees during the summer months, and no one was prepared for the sight that lay before them.

Row upon row of wooden barracks measuring about 20 feet by 120 feet greeted the detainees. One barrack housed four families, each living in an apartment about 20 feet by 24 feet. With plenty of gaping knotholes in the new lumber, dry, dusty winds swirled continuously into the buildings, not to mention the flies. No privacy existed since the walls of each apartment rose only part-way to the ceiling. No other accommodations were built within these shells. To eat, they had to stand in line at the mess hall. To shower or use the bathroom, they had to stand in line at latrines. To wash and iron clothes, they had to stand in line at the laundries. Recreation halls were built to monitor their leisure time. Shortly after arriving, the detainees were told they should expect to remain in this godforsaken place for up to six years.

Within Poston were three separate camps spaced about three to five miles apart. Ruth's family lived in Camp Three which held about five thousand people. Camp One, the largest, accommodated ten thousand; and

Camp Two another five thousand. Christened by the new residents as Camps Roasten, Toasten, and Dustin, the first death occurred fifteen days after the facility opened. Measles, polio, influenza, emphysema, tuberculosis, dysentery, and valley fever constantly threatened the population, and the suicide rate escalated above the national average.

In September 1943, Poston doctors determined seven-year-old Ruth should have her tonsils removed. When interviewed, Ruth explained how a trembling little girl tried her best to stay out of harm's way.

The thought of having my tonsils removed at the Post Camp I Hospital was terrifying. I remember the hospital room with small cots and other young children. A rumor was going around that a young boy had died after having his tonsils removed. I was petrified. The next morning as they were taking me to the operation room I remember holding my stomach real tight and staring at the ceiling.

Once in the operating room, the nurse placed the ether mask over my nose and mouth and told me to "breathe." I closed my eyes and held my breath silently counting to a hundred. When the nurse removed the mask, I let out my breath with a huge sigh! The nurse was upset and said, "No, no, you must breathe." I must have obeyed because I no longer have my tonsils.

Fear of what lay in store for them permeated the camps, affecting everyone from adults down to the smallest child, and Ruth was not exempt from the anxiety and fright each new day brought. The first time she saw an Indian ride hell-bent through camp chasing a wayward steer, she was so frightened that she later believed she had dreamed the incident. But Indians regularly rounded up stray cattle that wandered into the camps.

The threat of fire kept everyone watchful, particularly when hot plates came into use at the barracks and charcoal heaters were brought in to stave off cold winter winds that penetrated the ever-widening gaps in the walls.

One day, Ruth headed for an outside water faucet and found a rattlesnake curled up ready to pounce on its unsuspecting victim. She became so used to scorpions that she kept them as pets, pickling the poisonous creatures in alcohol and stockpiling them by her bed. Even at such a young age, she learned to make the best of her situation and take advantage of anything that came her

way, including pulling apart cotton balls to make yarn.
It's no wonder she was so excited about starting school.

The building Ruth entered that first day of school was
soon needed to house additional detainees. To expedite
construction of schoolhouses at the Poston campsites, an
adobe brick factory was established. The alkaline, sandy
soil prevalent in the Southwestern desert was perfect for
fashioning adobe bricks. Mixed with water and straw, the
thick concoction was poured into 12-by-18-by-4-inch
forms until set enough to remove, then left in the sun to
dry and harden for days, sometimes weeks, depending on
the weather. Everyone worked in the adobe factory
including school-age children. After spending their days
sitting in the dirt to do their lessons, they were motivated
to get the schoolhouses finished. By September 1943,
over five hundred thousand adobe bricks had been made,
enough to build schools in all three Poston camps.

Along with creating adobe bricks, the
men built wooden tables for the
schoolhouses, although each child
was expected to bring her own chair
from home. Eventually, books, paper,
and pencils began to arrive, usually

through the generosity of groups like the Quakers. And so at last, Ruth went to school.

Most of the teachers were Caucasian recruits, although Japanese American teachers and assistants also taught at Poston. For the first school year, 101 teaching positions were advertised. Seventy-two teachers showed up and two left immediately after seeing conditions at the camp. Twelve more left during the year. Nevertheless, a handful of teachers stayed the entire time the camp was open, and it was these teachers who made the greatest difference in the educational lives of Ruth and her classmates. Parents, however, were unhappy with the poor standards at the schools compared to those in California where their children excelled. Student/teacher ratios were double the national average.

Each morning the children sang "God Bless America" and recited the Pledge of Allegiance. Older students had their own version of the Pledge: ". . . with liberty and justice for all," they chanted, "—except us."

Many teachers lived on the outskirts of Poston, as did the majority of supervisors and guards, in the so-called "white" barracks: pristine framed, air-conditioned housing. A handful of teachers, however, preferred living in the "black barracks" situated in the middle of camp. These homes became havens where children could meet after school and talk about their fears and desires, and their anxious expectations for the future.

Since many of the families living at Poston were southern California farmers, they were expected to grow their own food in the dry, alkaline soil that blew uncontrollably across the desert. Fruits and vegetables, trees, flowers, even fishponds eventually flourished upon the harsh landscape, creating a semblance of beauty and the façade of a livable environment deep within Arizona's wasteland. The Japanese detainees also built an irrigation system that would later be expanded by the Office of Indian Affairs and used by the Colorado River Indian Tribe (CRIT) farmers.

For three long years, Ruth and her family endured the hardships of living in close confinement with thousands of other detainees, having no say in what they ate or where they worked, learning from outdated schoolbooks when they had any books at all, striving every day to create some sort of normal life. "The Japanese American detainees and the CRIT were pawns on the Poston game board," said Ruth years later, "with the hands of government officials moving groups of people about with no regard to the human dimensions of their actions."

Poston was not the only internment camp in Arizona. The state also housed the Gila River Relocation Camp, located about fifty miles southeast of Phoenix. In 1943, the President's wife, Eleanor Roosevelt, visited the Gila River Camp and wrote of her visit in an essay originally written for *Collier's Magazine*. Mrs. Roosevelt argued that as a nation, we could not be free to live our lives as we choose unless everyone enjoyed the same rights and privileges. It is too bad she was not in charge:

> *We have no common race in this country, but we have an ideal to which all of us are loyal: we cannot progress if we look down upon any group of people amongst us because of race or religion. Every citizen in this country has a right to our basic freedoms, to justice and to equality of opportunity. We retain the right to lead our individual lives as we please, but we can only do so if we grant to others the freedoms that we wish for ourselves.*

Eventually the United States Supreme Court determined that Japanese Americans could leave the camps anytime after January 2, 1945, and return to their homes.

On August 6 and again on August 9, 1945, the United States dropped atomic bombs on the cities of Hiroshima and Nagasaki, Japan, killing thousands of people and destroying entire villages. Within the month, on September 2, 1945—the war that was supposed to end all wars—ended.

By September 15, the Okimoto family was on their way back to San Diego. The State of California, however, protested the return of so many Japanese to its shores. Homeowners refused to relinquish houses once owned by Japanese families. Stores and other businesses now belonged to those who stepped in when the Japanese were forced to evacuate. Even Japanese fishing boats now sailed under the command of others.

When the Okimotos returned to the church they had established, they found an African-American congregation using the building. For almost a month, Ruth and her family lived in a small, one-room building behind the church with no kitchen or bathroom facilities. An upturned box served as their dining table, and Ruth watched cautiously as ants crawled over the ketchup bottle while she ate. Her father worked as a gardener while waiting for compensation and clothing promised by the War Relocation Authority (WRA). Unfortunately, the WRA ran out of money and the $200 they should have received never arrived. That December they accepted $87, all they would collect for three years of imprisonment.

The African-American congregation eventually relocated and the Okimotos settled back into the church facilities. The following year they moved to San Lorenzo near Oakland, California.

Through the years, Ruth continued her schooling and now holds a doctorate degree in organized psychology. She is also an accomplished artist and is active in the restoration of Poston as a memorial to those who turned the insufferable encampment into a viable agricultural community. "For a brief moment in history," said Ruth, "the Japanese American detainees experienced what the American Indians have endured for centuries."

The Office of Indian Affairs allowed the establishment of the Poston Internment Camp on reservation land with the idea that after the Japanese left, Native Americans would move onto the site. With an irrigation system in place and fields already producing crops, authorities promised not only the Mohave and Chemehuevi people, but also Navajo, Hopi, Apache, and other tribes they could occupy the barrack houses and farm the land.

Of the Native Americans who did relocate to Poston, many were grateful for the work of the Japanese in establishing arable soil across the harsh desert landscape. As one Hopi woman reiterated, "If it hadn't been for you Japanese people who figured out how to condition the soil in this valley and how to farm this land successfully, we wouldn't be here today!"

Ruth credits her involvement in the restoration of Poston with healing her childhood nightmares of living as a prisoner of war.

The opportunity to go deeper into the history of Poston changed my perception of those years. The revisit reduced the psychological and emotional pain I have carried for decades, and heightened my awareness of how government officials and their particular philosophies can impact groups of people. For the past three decades, I have used art as a way to deal with my camp experi-

ences. Drawing and painting helped unearth deep unconscious feelings about my childhood years in camp and its impact on my adult life.

Finally, Ruth was home.

ACKNOWLEDGMENTS

Writers are often viewed as loners, working long hours hunched over ink-stained tablets . . . or, in today's world, in front of glaring computer screens, researching faded manuscript pages, reading through ancient tomes, writing and rewriting. But alone, always alone. Yet nothing is farther from the truth.

I could not have completed the stories of these eleven amazing Arizona girls without the talented and capable assistance of the following individuals and organizations.

My dear friend and fellow historian Boyd Finch gave me the names of at least a dozen girls to start my research.

Historian Jim Turner at the Arizona Historical Society is always generous with his knowledge and expertise.

I want to thank Ruth Okimoto, who willingly shared her childhood years living at Poston Internment Camp.

Arizona Daily Star columnist Bonnie Henry gave me the idea for the story of Laurette Lovell. When I went looking for information on Laurette, Arizona Historical Society Museum Collections Manager Laraine Daly Jones presented me with a huge stack of material and was delighted that Laurette's story would finally be told.

ACKNOWLEDGMENTS

I appreciate the assistance of H. Christine Reid of the Pinal County Historical Society, Barbara Burton of the Prescott Valley Historical Society, Scott Anderson at Prescott's Sharlot Hall Museum archives, Ruth LeGate of Old Trails Museum in Winslow, and Mary Noon Kasualitis at the Arivaca Library.

In Flagstaff, Library Specialist Susan McGlothlin and Bee Valvo, Curator of Visual Materials at Northern Arizona University's Cline Library, became interested in my quest for information about Edith Jane Bass and provided invaluable research materials and photographs.

Arizona Softball Federation vice-president Karen Mischlispy and Joanna Burton of the Arizona Girls Softball Hall of Fame presented me with a profusion of stories and photographs depicting Arizona's softball girls. I also want to thank all the girls of summer who shared with me their teenaged memories of playing on two of the most famous women's softball teams in the country.

To good friends Tom and Dorothea Burke, thanks for putting me up and feeding me every time I appeared on your Prescott doorstep.

For support above and beyond, I want to give thanks and love to my family, especially my husband Bob, who allows me to rant and rave when I cannot find a missing piece of information, then dutifully reads my words and tells me I'm a genius.

BIBLIOGRAPHY

Bailey, Paul. *City in the Sun*. Los Angeles: Westernlore Press, 1971.

Barnes, Will C. *Arizona Place Names*. Tucson: University of Arizona Press, 1988.

Dichamp, Christiane Discher, ed. *Let Them Speak for Themselves: Women in the American West, 1849–1900*. Hamden, CT: Archon books, 1977.

Harris, Richard E. Harris. *The First 100 Years: A History of Arizona Blacks*. Apache Junction, AZ: Relmo Publishers, 1983.

James, George Wharton. *In and Around the Grand Canyon: The Grand Canyon of the Colorado River in Arizona*. Boston: Little, Brown, and Company, 1900.

James, Thomas. *Exile Within: The Schooling of Japanese Americans 1942–1956*. Cambridge, MA: Harvard University Press, 1987.

Katz, William Loren. *Black Women of the Old West*. New York: Atheneum Books for Young Readers, 1995.

Leavengood, Betty. *Lives Shaped: Grand Canyon Women by Landscape*. Boulder, CO: Pruett Publishing Company, 1999.

BIBLIOGRAPHY

Littlewood, Mary L. *Women's Fastpitch Softball—The Path to the Gold: An Historical Look at Women's Fastpitch in the United States.* Columbia, MO: National Fastpitch Coaches Association, 1998.

Luchetti, Cathy. *Children of the West: Family Life on the Frontier.* New York: W.W. Norton & Company, 2001.

Mauer, Stephen G. *Solitude & Sunshine: Images of a Grand Canyon Childhood.* Boulder, CO: Pruett Publishing Company, 1983.

Marriott, Barbara. *Annie's Guests: Tales from a Frontier Hotel.* Tucson: Catymatt Productions, 2002.

Martin, Patricia Preciado. *Songs My Mother Sang to Me.* Tucson: University of Arizona Press, 1992.

McGinty, Brian. *The Oatman Massacre: A Tale of Desert Captivity and Survival.* Norman: University of Oklahoma Press, 2005.

Miller, Joseph. *The Arizona Story.* New York: Hastings House, 1952.

Okimoto, Ruth Y. *Sharing a Desert Home: Life on the Colorado River Indian Reservation, Poston, Arizona, 1942–1945.* Berkeley, CA: Heyday Books, 2001.

Protas, Josh. *A Past Preserved in Stone: A History of Montezuma Castle National Monument.* Tucson: Western National Parks Association, 2002.

BIBLIOGRAPHY

Sheridan, Thomas E. *Arizona: A History*. Tucson: University of Arizona Press, 1995.

Smith, Dean. *The Fains of Lonesome Valley*. Prescott Valley, AZ: Lonesome Valley Press, 1998.

Sonnichen, C.L. *Tucson: The Life and Times of an American City*. Norman: University of Oklahoma Press, 1982.

Stratton, Emerson Oliver and Edith Stratton Kitt. *Pioneering in Arizona: The Reminiscences of Emerson Oliver Stratton and Edith Stratton Kitt*. John Alexander Carroll, ed. Tucson AZ: Arizona Pioneers' Historical Society, 1964.

Stratton, R.B. *Captivity of the Oatman Girls*. Lincoln: University of Nebraska Press, 1983. Originally published: New York: Carlton & Porter, 1857.

Udall, Louise. *Me and Mine: The Life Story of Helen Sekaquaptewa*. Tucson: University of Arizona Press, 1969.

Wagoner, Jay J. *Early Arizona: Prehistory to Civil War*. Tucson: University of Arizona Press, 1975.

Wilbur-Cruce, Eva Antonia. *A Beautiful, Cruel Country*. Tucson: University of Arizona Press, 1987.

PHOTO CREDITS

Page 1: Portrait of Olive Ann Oatman taken after the Mohaves released her from captivity, 1857. Yale Collection of Americana, Beinecke Rare Book and Manuscript Library, Yale University. Page 18: Atanacia Santa Cruz Hughes, with husband Sam and daughter Lizzie in 1867. Courtesy of the Arizona Historical Society/Tucson, AHS#26851. Page 36: Laurette Lovell at about age 20. Courtesy of the Arizona Historical Society/Tucson. Page 50: Anna Box Neal, date unknown. Courtesy of the Arizona Historical Society/Tucson, AHS#61970. Page 66: Edith Olive Stratton. Courtesy of the Arizona Historical Society/Tucson, AHS#63821. Page 82: Ruth Sill after milking cow, 1907. Sharlot Hall Museum Photo. Prescott, Arizona. Page 95: Edith Jane Bass feeding chickens, 1910. Image courtesy of Cline Library, Northern Arizona University. Page 110: Young Indian girls weaving baskets, Village of Shipauiovi, Hopi Indian Reservation, Arizona, circa 1903. Library of Congress Prints and Photographs Division, LC-USZ62-50345. Page 127: Eva Antonia Wilbur-Cruce, age 13. Courtesy of the Arizona Historical Society/Tucson, AHS#97391. Page 143: 1935 PBSW Ramblers. Courtesy of Arizona Softball Hall of Fame, Prescott, Arizona. Page 161: Self-portrait of Ruth Okimoto. "Summer 1942" Oil on canvas, 22" x 30", 1985. Courtesy of Ruth Okimoto.

ABOUT THE AUTHOR

Jan Cleere has distinguished herself in the field of historical nonfiction by tirelessly pursuing long-forgotten manuscripts, tear-stained diaries, and old-timers with a story to tell, relentlessly looking for elusive ghosts from the past. She is the author of two other award-winning Globe Pequot books: *More Than Petticoats: Remarkable Nevada*  *Women* (2005), and *Outlaw Tales of Arizona: True Stories of Arizona's Most Famous Robbers, Rustlers, and Bandits* (2006). Jan holds a writing degree in American Studies and lives in Oro Valley, Arizona.